MW01035932

TRIBAL F*CKS UP DIGITAL
Discover the Blind Spots that sabotage Digital Adoption
and derail your Business Process Transformation

©2023 Klaus Imping
contact@klausimping.com | klausimping.com

Hardcover ISBN: 978-1-947276-22-2
Paperback ISBN: 978-1-947276-27-7
eBook ISBN: 978-1-947276-20-8

Publisher:

Epic Author Publishing
4437 Roanoak Way
Palm Harbor, FL 34685, United States of America
info@epicauthor.com

Ordering Information:

Quantity sales. Special discounts are available on quantity purchases by corporations, associations, and others. For details, contact the author or the publisher.

First Edition; Released April 2023

TRIBAL F*CKS UP DIGITAL

Discover the **Blind Spots** that sabotage Digital Adoption and derail your Business Process Transformation.

Klaus Imping
Michael Ciatto

We believe the magic switch to make
digital transformation successful is a simple one.

We believe this switch is not technology or
deep functional expertise, no rocket science.

We believe YOU are the one who can turn that switch.

We believe YOU can make the difference and will
leave your footsteps on the change path of your organization.

This might be an inflection point, YOUR **Kairos***.

KAIROS was the Greek god of the moment, while Chronos was the god of sequential time.
In rhetoric, ***Kairos is known as the decisive moment, the passing instant when an
opening appears which must be seized with force if success is to be achieved.**

"Kairos 2'23" by the German artist Bruno Wank
www.brunowank.de
© VG Bild-Kunst, Bonn (Germany) 2023

Preface

TECHNOLOGY MUST ADVANCE FREEDOM

Technology Must Advance Freedom is the principle on which the Krach Institute for Tech Diplomacy was founded. While running US economic diplomacy, it became abundantly clear to me that technology can be used for good or evil. I have witnessed firsthand how authoritarian regimes use today's technology to create a surveillance state with the destructive power that the worst of dictators could have only dreamed of.

The reality we face as a nation and the free world is one of ever-increasing cyber warfare and seemingly ceaseless variations of intense weaponized techno-economic competition. Both sides of the aisle truly understand that our rivals are playing the long game and they are playing for keeps — a four-dimensional game of economic, military, diplomatic, and cultural chess. Worst of all, they have little respect for human rights, intellectual property, rule of law, transparency, the environment, or the sovereignty of other nations. In this epic struggle between freedom and authoritarianism, technology is at the crossroads and its main battleground.

During my tenure at the U.S. State Department, I came to see how vital the private sector is in preserving freedom. From my previous roles as an entrepreneur and CEO, I understand how critical technology is for companies to preserve their own freedom. The freedom of companies is derived from the Constitution, but it depends on profitability, competitive advantage, and sustainability. Advancing freedom is about transformational leadership and adeptly using technology for exactly these purposes.

My life's work has been focused on creating innovative companies by building high-performance teams that challenge the status quo and then empowering them to pursue opportunities and accomplish things they never imagined possible. I believe the team with the best people wins, and that diversity of thought is the catalyst *for genius.*

The digital transformation is upon us. It is characterized by a fusion of technologies that is blurring the lines between the physical, digital, and biological spheres. The geometric nature of these transformations is best understood by the fact that it took radio thirty-eight years and television thirteen years to reach audiences of fifty million people. On the other hand, it took the internet only four years, the iPod three years, and Facebook two years to do the same. In its essence, the digital transformation is very simple: organizations are connecting everyone, everything, everywhere, all the time. They are becoming capable of delivering instant, intimate, frictionless, incremental value on a large scale and are creating a world in which people, insights, and money interact quickly, easily, and cheaply.

What is enabling the transformation is that rarest of things, a genuine paradigm shift in leadership. Firms leading the digital transformation are being run vastly different from the unwieldy industrial behemoths of the twentieth century. Their transformational leaders are focused on continuous innovation for customers, and have organized their firms to be nimble, adaptable, and able to adjust on the fly to meet the shifting whims of a marketplace driven by end-users. Think Amazon, Apple, Facebook, Google, Microsoft, Tesla, Airbnb, Shopify, Atlassian, Salesforce, Samsung, Spotify, DocuSign, and SpaceX. For them, the future is thrilling and uplifting.

For the "unenlightened" organizations that continue to be run like the lumbering twentieth century mastodons, the situation is extremely different. Examples are abundant. It's no surprise that fewer than one hundred of the companies in the S&P 500 stock index were around when that index began.

The crucial insights that Klaus and Michael provide on this challenge include not only the practical experience that drops out of every page, but the unconventional, and sometimes non-intuitive ways to uncover and address critical issues, culminating in the simple advice of *"Get it right or leave it. Anything else is waste."*

What I find useful is that Klaus and Michael do not just describe the problem and its symptoms, but they provide a clear idea for what *right* is and a prescriptive strategy for *getting it right*. It's fresh thinking, a different perspective, relevant, and a worthwhile read for any CxO, senior manager, and digitalization executive.

I wish you all the best in your transformational journey and pass on my heartfelt gratitude for advancing freedom through the skillful use of trusted technology.

The Honorable Keith J. Krach

Former U.S. Under Secretary of State; Chairman and CEO of Ariba and DocuSign; Vice President of General Motors; Chairman Emeritus of Purdue University; 2022 Nobel Peace Prize Nominee

Table of Contents

Executive Summary

Why is it that about 70 percent of all digital transformations fail to achieve their objectives?

It all comes down to one thing. Tribal elements.

Those who experience digital transformation failure are essentially failing to dissect and overcome the tribal elements of a company's processes. When we say *tribal*, we mean the distinct knowledge and processes that employees use on their own accord to get the job done.

They use their own knowledge, self-developed process, and tools of comfort, typically spreadsheets, as opposed to a clearly defined, documented, universally trained and holistically adopted process, primed for continuous, systematic improvement, and transition to future owners.

> Tribal ways of working neutralize the effectiveness of any digitally transformed to-be state. Neutralized effectiveness means neutralized return.
>
> Money, time, energy — all invested for **nothing**.

More and more CEOs and CFOs are frustrated with poor effectiveness and low returns on investments in digital transformation. The bigger the investment and more strategic the initiative, the more blinding the spotlight becomes for sponsors and executives in charge. No one wants to be asked, "How did you spend XX million and fail to get it right?"

The crucial question is **how to avoid tribal ways of working.** As a leader of a transformation project, how can you rid the enterprise of disconnected work-arounds, local and offline spreadsheets, and dependency on individual knowledge when your true intention is to achieve a digitalized, transformed, new process environment? Tribal ways of working sit directly in conflict with this agenda.

The answer is surprisingly simple: Start with defining the process and focus intently on **workflows**.

Let's use a simple analogy to explain this viewpoint. Over the last few decades, the world has seen a tremendous change in design and management of material flow processes. In the light of lean, The Toyota Way, 6 Sigma, etc., every step, movement, turn, and tool gets exactly designed and fine-tuned. The interplay of subprocesses gets synchronized and the avoidance of waste justifies detailed conceptual efforts. Continuous improvement is an immanent knock-on impact.

It's common sense that these principles are state-of-the-art for material flow processes. But why stop there? **Why isn't this established best practice applied to information flow processes?**

There is only one aspect that is more surprising than the fact that these principles do not get applied, and that is the common expectation of good results without the application of those principles. Quite naive, isn't it?

But it's simpler said than done — *putting much more focus on workflows.*

The **paradigms** that the business world typically applies to optimizing, changing, and digitally transforming, are quite technology- and **system-centric.**

The approach is rarely cross functional, hence the opportunity to define a transformative, integrated operating model is wasted. There are many mechanisms, patterns, and behaviors that prevent the process and workflow topic from rising to the forefront of a digital transformation.

As we will discuss, these distractors range from tool-centric paradigms, the role of IT organizations, the software vendor and system integrator influence, internal resistance, and above all the mis-calibration of strategic mindsets.

YOU, as a leader, or key stakeholder and influencer **are in demand here**. Don't expect your organization to find its way out on its own. It needs your kick!

The key to successful digital transformation is not finding the newest, shiniest system to integrate, but defining a visionary, transformative to-be operating model that encompasses a holistic scope and then implementing it with a process-first and workflow-centric mindset, enabled by the best fitting technology.

Don't expect a new, transformative operating model to result from a system implementation. Your new, transformed operating model sets the frame and determines supporting technology. **That's the paradigm shift.**

In order to make that shift, top-management initiative and continuous attention are vital. That's the only way to get it right — to make digital transformation sustainably effective.

Transformation must be business led. IT and procurement have supporting and facilitating roles. Our decades of experience with global enterprises and self-reflection within many of these organizations reveal this is the exception rather than the norm.

Without shifting the paradigm from technology-led to business-led, the result is predictable: **Tribal sabotages digital.**

Does this already resonate with you? Does it trigger an urging gut instinct or maybe even heighten some unspoken concerns? If so, follow your gut — **go to *Conclusion* on page 269 ff. right away**, and read the rest afterward!

Introduction

The rate at which technology has advanced and evolved has outpaced the rate of process optimization. Why?

My personal experience is based on a decade in the industry and over twenty-five years in process consulting, predominantly in the magic triangle of business processes, information technology and change for improvement. My primary focus was and is on value streams and supply chain management in complex networks and business environments, often in manufacturing and service industries in manifold markets, sectors, products, and business typologies.

I've seen and lived through many hypes and waves — some real innovations giving impulses, many just hollow buzzwords. I managed to make projects and initiatives successful, and I have also failed here and there.

True experience results from wins and losses.

I have interviewed nearly one hundred CxO's and senior management representatives across different industries in preparation for this book. What I heard confirmed my suspicion that some things have not really changed in the last thirty years. Hence, I think it's important to give you some background on my path of experience that has impacted and shaped my perspective on digital business process transformation.

I am a member of the late Boomer, early Gen-X generation, and I hit the business world in the late '80s and early '90s. Depending on your age, you may remember the CIM-hype — computer-integrated manufacturing. CIM was sort of the first broader attempt at end-to-end digitalization, if you will. That was my era when I entered this business world.

Even though the CIM idea triggered enormous progress and improvements in certain areas, especially the process section between construction and production, from computer-aided design (CAD) to computer-aided manufacturing (CAM), the broader vision of holistic integration and full automation never came true.

The Era of "Process" in the '90s

What followed the CIM-hype was very sobering for technology enthusiasts. The mid-'90s were dominated by the word *process*. Michael Hammer and James Champy created a business management hype around "Business Process Reengineering" when they launched their bestselling book *Reengineering the Corporation: A Manifesto for Business Revolution.*[1]

It was 1993, and the book became one of the three most important business books of the past twenty years by none other than Forbes[2]. Key messages like "Don't automate, obliterate"[3] struck the tech-believing world. By defining "process" as "a set of activities that, taken together, produce a result of value to the customer," a new perspective found its way into business.

All of a sudden, someone dared to ask, "which activities belong together?" and "why are we doing this?" instead of "how can we optimize and automate it?" and "what technology to use?"

Talk about a hard time for technology evangelists.

---

1 Reengineering the Corporation: A Manifesto for Business Revolution, Hammer, M. and Champy, J., Harper Collins, New York, 1993
2 "The 20 Most Influential Business Books," Forbes, September 30, 2002
3 "Reengineering Work: Don't Automate, Obliterate," Michael Hammer, Harvard Business Review, July, 1990

"Businesses had to be willing to look across and beyond functional departments to processes — no easy task in corporations that had been for years committed to traditional methods of organization."[4]

This statement was formulated in 1993. Could it be more up to date?

Thank God, the internet and the .COM boom brought us back to where we had been before. Technology.

The Return of the Technology Belief

Today, any smartphone has more computing power than a mainframe in the eighties.

Indeed, technology improved massively. It has become exponentially more powerful — the internet connects everything and everyone.

Systems, databases, cloud computing, artificial intelligence, machine learning — the spectrum of powerful and affordable technology that is available to digitalize business processes is fairly unlimited at this point.

And yet, there is a significant discrepancy between the tremendous progress in technology compared to the relatively little progress in process integration.

---

4 Reengineering the Corporation: A Manifesto for Business Revolution, Hammer, M. and Champy, J., Harper Collins, New York, 1993

The rate at which technology has advanced and evolved has outpaced the rate of process optimization in the average organization. It has resulted in businesses conforming their processes to fit technology, rather than taking time to find technology that compliments and supports existing processes. Processes, might I add, that very well could be or generate a company's competitive advantage.

Is it just my subjective impression? I don't think so.

Recent studies from Bain,[5] BCG,[6] McKinsey,[7] and others, e. g. independent industry research like Zippia Research,[8] on success rates of digital transformations state that only 30 percent or even less of transformations succeed in achieving their objectives. These studies are all from different sources across different timelines and different companies, and yet, they all concluded the same thing:

There is a poor success rate when it comes to digital transformation.

This book is here to guide you away from being on the wrong side of that statistic. Think about it.

---

5 "Orchestrating a Successful Digital Transformation," Bain & Company 2017
6 "Unlocking Success in Digital Transformations," McKinsey & Company 2018
7 "Flipping the Odds of Digital Transformation Success," Boston Consulting Group 2020
8 "37 Digital Transformation Statistics [2022]: Need-To-Know Facts On The Future Of Business," Sky Ariella, Zippia.com. Apr. 26, 2022, https://www.zippia.com/advice/digital-transformation-statistics/

Our Ambition

Regarding relevance and magnitude of experience, the same applies to my co-author Michael Ciatto. He is not only a friend, but an "alter ego" in terms of thinking about digital process transformation. Our thought process, experiences, and vision align better than most people I have ever met.

For years, Michael has been a respected industry peer and competitor in providing global enterprises process-led transformation services. In numberless engagements, Michael has helped executive leadership teams reset their mindset to be process focus first, correctly view analytics and digital tools as enablers, and most critically reset their operating model to support strategic business initiatives and be viable across diverse macroeconomic and industry dynamics. The key paradigm behind these solutions is the unwavering belief that processes tied to corporate strategic objectives must drive the requirements and the subsequently developed use cases should be the only evaluation criteria for defining, selecting, and deploying digital tools.

I am grateful to co-author this book with someone with such vast experience and strategic thinking as Michael. Between his and my experience and our ongoing research and collaboration with executives across the globe, it's safe to say that the thoughts, ideas, and messages of this book are broadly applicable across all industries.

Our joint ambition is no less than igniting a paradigm shift in digital business process transformation.

Based on both our own observations and the recent studies from leading consulting firms, it's been proven that there is a low success rate of digital transformation. Regardless of the study publisher, Gartner, Forbes, McKinsey, to name a few, the failure rate is greater than that of a professional baseball pitcher; meaning you have less than a 30 percent probability of realizing your vision and the associated business case to justify the investment.

The only difference, failure is expected in baseball, even a 30 percent success rate lands you in the Hall of Fame. A 30 percent success rate in business spells lots of wasted time, energy, and shareholder value.

Big promises, huge expectations, little impact.

This is appalling given the importance of digitalization and digital transformation in the success of a business in this century. Nobody doubts that this has the magnitude of the next industrial revolution. As we look to the next generation of the workforce, ingrained digital solutions are just a natural part of the expectation. So, how could it be that more than two-thirds of companies fail in their pursuit of digital, technology-enabled transformation?

What is even more annoying nowadays, despite use case after use case of failed initiatives, is the persistent excitement and belief that technology in and of itself holds the answer.

There is a paradigm shift that needs to occur that takes business leaders away from focusing on "digital", technology-led solutions while expecting organizational and operational "transformation" as a result. It simply doesn't work that way.

The business world has technology blinders on, and neither the software vendors nor most "consultants" have any interest in pulling those blinders off. It's their money machine, why would they? Even if these parties were indescribably altruistic actors, they do not understand nor have the ability to convey to leadership — and more importantly, the "mighty middle" — how to plan successfully, execute and sustain a digitally enabled transformation.

The **technology paradigm is mainstream**, and it's truly hard to compete with mainstream thinking. The capabilities, buzzwords, and art of the possible are inspiring and attention grabbing, who has time to pause to think through the nuances and gritty details of operationalizing true transformation?

As a result, many digitalization and digital transformation initiatives experience poor adoption, miss their targets, and ultimately fail. The pitfalls are as simple as they are similar — common patterns everywhere. It sucks, and the only way past it is to take the blinders off and become aware of the root cause behind digital transformation failure.

So, what do you do if you clearly see that the mainstream paradigm needs to be changed? What do you do if you know that it doesn't require rocket science to make an impactful influence on the results your company will see through digitalization?

It's simple.

You can wait for others to stand up, or you can stand up. Our "standing up" materialized in the decision to write *Tribal F*cks up Digital*. In the pages ahead, we will share our point of view with you as you learn about the nuances in leading and executing a successful digital business process transformation. And just to warn you — we will loudly question the mainstream paradigm the majority seem to have fallen into.

The key message is, in summary, simple —

Business leaders need to change their paradigm from technology- and system-centricity to business-process-centricity.

Technology and systems are just the means to an end, enablers of new ways of working. The end, the purpose, is the business process, embedded in a digitally enabled, new operating model, empowering the workforce of the future.

WORKFLOW FIRST, technology second.

Given the importance of digitalization, given the fact that we are now in the next industrial revolution, given the continuous progress and innovation happening in information technology, and given the vast amount of mature technology offerings and vendors — the poor success rate is more than surprising. It's unacceptable.

There's clearly something systematically wrong. What is it?

The answer is – of course – not unidimensional.

Hence, there is no simplified silver bullet that will fix it. Many aspects contribute to the low adoption rates when a new technology is integrated into an organization's operating model. Many of these aspects are part of the answer that you usually get:

....

Data

People

Change Management

Senior Management Engagement

But there is a missing link, and it's the one aspect that people rarely talk about.

The Missing Link

Whether it's CIM for the early nineties or today's Industry 4.0, digitalization, digital transformation, the problem remains the same. It always starts with *digital* when it should start with *workflow*.

Business leaders have developed the habit of pushing their operational issues into the technology drawer thinking, "It's a technological challenge. Information technology, systems will fix it."

Projects and programs are approached from a "technology implementation"-perspective. The world is in extreme excitement about artificial intelligence (AI) and machine learning (ML) with a deep belief in software vendors' overkilling marketing yell that tech and systems resolve everything.

Along with this technology- and system-centric mindset, the dimension of process and workflow has lost focus and attention. But this is where the rubber meets the road.

A new operating model is the true object of digitalization.

Don't get us wrong, we are not questioning the importance of technology at all. Information technology is essential. It even offers opportunities to design processes and workflows in a disruptive way. Without technological innovation, it would be unattainable. So, while essential, it is still just an enabler.
As the business world aims to drive micro-innovation, operate at the edge and democratize innovation, the most critical truth must not be lost: At the heart of innovation and transformation is still people.

> The **workflow** is the **missing link** to **connect people, technology, and business purpose.**

Imagine we would apply the same depth and attention to the design of information processes and its workflows as we do for the design of material flow processes. The principles of Lean, 6 Sigma, Toyota's industry-changing production system — they are transferable to information flows. Why don't we apply it?

This is a critical omission — it's a **blind spot** — it's the missing link.

Maybe we think systems and technology will do this for us instead. They will not! No system with its "out-of-the-box" resources will guide the way or even deliver a new operating model. The new operating model is the starting point, and detailing its information processes needs attention and purposeful design down to the workflow level. In this respect, this book is supposed to be like Hammer's and Champy's revolutionary wake-up call in the nineties.

Let's shift paradigms from technology-and-system-centric to process-and-workflow-centric digitalization approaches.

Operating model, process, and workflow first, and technology second.

It's On You!

Again: Our joint ambition is no less than igniting a paradigm shift in digital business process transformation.

This paradigm shift is materialized in the Kairos image.

YOU can be the **crystal nucleus** in your organization.

If you have the power, then start now. If you don't, look for allies.

But, no matter what, it's time to think differently. In the post-COVID-19 world, successful digital-enabled transformation is no longer a luxury, rather is it a necessity for corporate survival. It's time to start. **Now!**

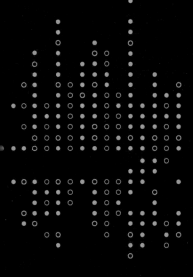

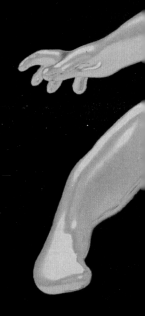

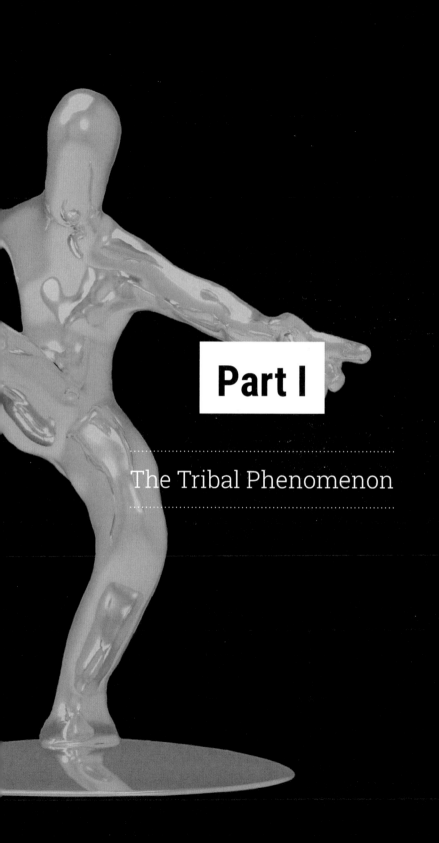

Part I

The Tribal Phenomenon

.

Klaus' Background Story - The Proof That Process Is Key

You can cure bad tools with good processes, but not bad processes with good tools.

Quite early in my career, I had a pretty unique opportunity. It was 1990. Keep in mind — the Berlin Wall that was separating East and West Germany, as well as the fast-developing West from the socialist, central planned Eastern world, fell in 1989.

The Western German corporation that I had joined a few years before, a world-leading industrial gears manufacturer, was one of the first who acquired an East German production factory once the wall fell. Under the Eastern German regime, this factory (with its nearly 2,000 employees) was part of a state combine. The combine consisted of seven production sites across the territories of the former "German Democratic Republic" and employed over 7,000 people. It was truly a multi-site enterprise of decent size with an extensive production network. Quite complex.

How To Manage Complexity Without IT?

At that time, East Germany's information technology (IT) capabilities were comparable to western standards in the 1960s. Sequenced batch processing, information manually recorded on punched tape, seven online terminals and removable hard disks with less capacity than any SD card of fingernail size has today.

Processing cycles for operational information flows like order entry, bill of material maintenance, material requirements calculation, etc., were done weekly in the best case.

Also worth mentioning, there was no internet. We did not have data lines connecting the different production sites. Any and all data transfers took place physically, by bringing data media from point A to point B.

Fun facts aside, the factory had heavy machinery. Equipped with a foundry, hardening shop and die sinking milling machines that could form gears of two meters in diameter. In this factory environment, IT was the second biggest power consumer with more than one hundred single devices that were producing more heat than information processing power.

So, in summary, information technology was not suspected to be the driving force for information flow processes.

Process and Discipline

Yet, initially extra surprising to me, there were no master data problems. Even though master data had to grow up and be maintained across seven separate sites, joint numbering systems had to be kept integer. The construction design and engineering process had to cater for technical standardization — reinforced by the eastern economy of scarcity — which needs a lot of coordination.

No master data problems. Data was complete. Data was consistent.

What was the success factor to achieve this?

Obviously, it was not information technology. The uniqueness of this extreme example is to take technology completely out of the picture.

If we do that, what is left as the success factor to achieve master data quality without the support of information technology? The answer is simple: **the process.**

This Eastern German combine organization had a strict regime of processes, workflows, and standard operating procedures. The sequence of actions, the information inputs requested, its formats, the responsibilities who was in charge to provide them, the cut-off times until when input had to be delivered, this was all precisely designed, described, and implemented. The result was a cross-functional orchestration that worked like clockwork. Process adherence, which was probably also ingrained in the culture, played a large part in this. It's no surprise in an environment where everything depends on the process. Yet it makes a crucial success factor obvious: human adoption and buy-in. Success and effectiveness are dependent on unquestioned commitment to the process and defined responsibilities across the entire workflow.

From Technology to Efficiency: The Missing Link

One would expect that this level of efficiency and structure in an operating model can only be acquired by injecting technology support.

Really? I don't think so.

This seems to be a common problem today across the board. Organizations think that technology will bring process efficiency. Rather, it's your processes that should lead the charge.

Take something as simple as master data — companies that claim good master data quality seem to be an absolute exception. The vast majority of companies admit master data quality as a problem, at least as a serious concern, when it comes to digitalization.

In my nearly one hundred interviews with CxOs and senior management representatives from different companies in different segments and industries, there was one main commonality I heard from many of these leaders — "Poor master data quality".

Why do such problems exist?

Lack of supporting information technology can be excluded as a potential root cause. You could have the fanciest, most expensive enterprise resource planning (ERP), "Master Data Hub" or master data management (MDM) tool on the market. In fact, all companies in this day and age have more modern and advanced systems, connectivity, real-time processing and visibility compared to my Eastern German example from above, without question. And to be fair, they have spent decades and tens of millions of dollars on these solutions and the associated system implementations.

And yet, the vast majority of my interviewees still complained about their company's poor master data quality. They still struggle to find that special oil that makes the machine run smoothly and efficiently, even after they spend ample capital to improve it.

How? Why?

> This exactly brings us to the central thesis of my discovery, the missing link for effective digital transformation — **Processes.**

But, when you look at a company's processes, you will see an interwoven web of operations that make the company tick. When you zoom in to a more granular view, there is a more detailed level of a process that serves as the link to the vault of digitalization success. Without this link tightly chained to the people and operations of an organization, a new system will only be a shiny object rather than a means of amplifying operational efficiency. Without a properly defined operating model with clear responsibility and adoption monitoring, the new system will stale quickly and be worked around frequently.

Too often, this link is not evaluated, considered, and understood.

The missing link is the WORKFLOW!

The Nature of Tribal Business Processes – A Comprehensive Overview

Tribal workflows are like tribal knowledge: they cause a lotus effect on any improvement — including digitalization.

Tribal knowledge is a commonly known phenomenon and used expression. It describes information and know-how that is only resident in the mind of a single person or group. More often than not, this knowledge evolved in the confines of the existing company and its legacy operations. The knowledge, or stagnation of its evolution, is further engrained through continued reinforcement of training and onboarding programs.

The problem with tribal knowledge is that it's, well, tribal. It's known by the tribe and only the tribe that works on it. It's not easily duplicatable because it's not documented and thus, not accessible to others. There's no way to verify, update, or teach unless it is done so by someone from the tribe.

Equally troubling is the harsh reality that challenging and improving tribal knowledge and processes is nearly infeasible. Comfort comes with tribal processes that are known to the existing team and are often credited with prior career successes. This in combination with the tenacity of the crowd makes it an uphill battle to challenge tribal processes. Lastly, the lack of documentation, systematic enablement, and accessibility of data makes it difficult to demonstrate the shortcomings of existing tribal practices in a quantified way.

What if someone from the tribe leaves the team? What if you have a new hire and the tribe is unable to train them? What if you want to implement technology to streamline the processes and increase efficiencies within a given sector, but parts or all of the process are held close to the chest of those who run the show?

Sure, tribal knowledge is problematic from a corporate perspective. But what's more problematic are the tribal processes — more specifically, the tribal workflows. A *workflow* is the detailed, operationally executed level of a business process — the level where the work flows.

Tribal processes and workflows have a similar nature to tribal knowledge in the sense that they are:

- Not documented

- Not accessible

- Not verifiable

- Difficult to update

- Hard to teach

- Nearly impossible to challenge with hard data

The famous local Excel spreadsheet is probably the most obvious symptom of a tribal workflow. Tools, methods, and logic are kept at a local, individual level. In this scenario, collaboration and interaction with others do not follow explicit rules. They just happen, either by occasion or by habit.

The opposite of "tribal" in this context is "explicit" in the sense of being purposefully structured, documented, and trained in such a way that the lived process corresponds to the desired process.

Every corporation has countless tribal workflows.

Few are known, most are hidden. For some, it's not problematic at all. Processes that happen occasionally, are not time critical, and are not impactful don't cause as big of a ripple effect when they stay tribal. But many tribal workflows are repetitive, impactful, time critical, and business critical. Even more troubling are those processes that must integrate and orchestrate activity across different functional teams, being also reliant on tribal workflows. This further complicates the ability to drive harmonization across the enterprise and to respond to disruptions in a timely manner with data-driven insights and fast decision-making across silos.

This is where we should focus.

It's not just about the risks and problems that tribal workflows entail.

> **Tribal workflows are hiding from process improvement.**
> They hide from digitalization, from automation. Tribal sabotages digital.

This makes them so dangerous on one hand, but also a gold mine for business value creation on the other. It's a two-sided coin.

Appearances of Tribal Workflows

Some may say, "We do have well-described and documented process-es, this tribal-thing doesn't apply to us."

Ha! That might be the case, but tribal processes are often hidden and difficult to detect. They may be hiding right under your nose without your attention.

> Check out the "three easy and quick litmus tests to iden-tify tribal workflows" in the section "Privileged Access to Supporting Ressources."

Let's approach them by classifying them into three groups:

1. Camouflaged Tribal Workflows

2. Broken Tribal Workflows

3. Blind Spot Tribal Workflows

Camouflaged Tribal Workflows

These workflows are those where an explicit process design exists. They are well designed and documented, for example, as a necessary part of a quality management system.

However, the process description ends at a level of specificity that only indicatively describes the flow. It's not detailed nor granular enough, in short, it leaves enough leeway to operate the real-life practical workflow very differently. Without tight systematic controls, the rigor, consistency, and cycle time of the process and workflows, it's unpredictable if not random.

I sat down with the global head of planning processes of a European pharmaceuticals manufacturer, undergoing a huge program to transform their supply chain planning digitally. He said, "To-be-state processes were designed on Level 3. We leave it to the operational folks how they apply it."

My concern would not be how they apply it, but if at all. Good luck with adoption. The challenge is that Level 3 designs allow for enough flexibility that innovative operators can find a means to work-around the intended flow. Often the design process stops at Level 3 initially because the concepts are largely not disputed or overly argumentative at this level. It is when driven down to detail level 4 and 5 workflows that resistance arises, and the real scope and magnitude of change management is revealed. Level 3 doesn't hurt!

Broken Tribal Workflows

The broken tribal workflows are partially explicit, partially tribal. The explicit piece typically exists within a silo. For example, it could exist within a certain business function like customer service, equipped with a proper support system, processes purposefully designed, linked with process-supporting system functionality — basically what you would expect from a well-organized process.

But it's just a segment of the end-to-end. The real **end-to-end workflow** goes across the boundaries of this business function and of the supporting system. Let's look at an example of a vendor-managed inventory (VMI) process case, a medical device manufacturer taking care of the inventory at its hospital or distributor customers and providing supply as needed. While the classical process allows work in silos — the customer does inventory management and raises an order to get supply — the vendor-managed inventory setup goes across traditional silo borders and requires orchestrated interaction that must be highly collaborative, cross-function, and cross-system, cross-enterprise to realize success.

This is where explicit workflows often break.

The supply chain vice president of another big European manufactur-er of medical consumables talked about a pilot project for digitalized VMI to hospitals in one European country. Their intention was to use storage containers with weighing systems in the hospitals and have it send an alert when a certain weight and quantity were trending to-ward or registered below a set limit. This alert signal then resulted in an email to customer service. And guess what, the rest of the process was manual.

Wow.

Unfortunately, this is not an uncommon, one-off outlier.

In a similar situation, one of the largest CPG clients in the world was working to fully digitalize their latest manufacturing plant. The investment exceeded over fifty million dollars and considered every state-of-art tooling and technology capability. A full deployment of a new manufacturing execution system (MES), inline IoT sensors, and even robotic line loading and product warehousing made this a lead-ing example of fully digitalized manufacturing.

At the end of this impressive operation stood over a half dozen work-ers, some with laptops and some with pens and paper. When asked their role in the process, the SVP of Global Operations lost the gleam-ing pride that covered his face. He softly sighed and gently lowered his eyes to the floor and said, "They are recording the production outs to transfer these manually into our planning and customer service platforms."

In the excitement of completely reengineering the manufacturing processes, the critical integration points and information transfer to tangential teams and processes were forgotten.

The lesson: the solution resolved a problem for a function, not for the enterprise. Vertical thinking was applied, not horizontal.

We'll get to that point later.

Blind Spot Tribal Workflows

These workflows are not explicit at all, not on the workflow level nor on a higher level of process description. They are left to the improvisation and creativity of the actors, and often simply habits that emerged over time.

Processes that deal with exceptions, managing variations and disruptions do often show tribal nature. COVID-19 was a great detector of tribal processes and workflows. As volatility and disruptions rose to an all-time high, all the buffers (such as inventory) were drained, and the flaws in the process were exposed. The heightened level of agility required to operate in the environment showed the warts of processes that were reliant on human intervention, embedded latencies, and lack of scalability.

Ad hoc, unscripted, case by case.

The digitalization-team of a manufacturer of refined metal products recently demonstrated the results of their "Industry 4.0" efforts regarding real-time visibility of their production processes. They showcased an impressive breadth of information, close to real-time, presented through a modern and user-friendly interface.

The question regarding who makes use of this information and how was responded with, "We offer it to our organization to make use of it." After some poking, they complemented with "But we don't know if and how they do it."

This led into an exiting discussion about the end point of digitalization with the consensus that it must be the purposeful use of digital enablement, not just its provisioning.

How to Uncover Tribal Workflows? The Symptoms and Red Flag Warnings

Camouflaged tribal workflows are the most difficult to detect. Without the comparison between the explicit version and the practiced version, you won't detect them. It takes intention and due diligence. A point of discovery we often see is the attempt to apply automation to certain workflow steps, for example using robotic process automation (RPA). When evolving to testing the automation, users unavoidably highlight that the workflows in practice do not resemble those documented in the explicit version.

Broken tribal workflows are typically identifiable by manual interaction. This includes:

- Information exchange via email or shared drive
- The famous local Excel spreadsheet that was already mentioned
- Phone or verbal communication
- Meetings

Wherever you see any of these symptoms, it's a clear suspicion that a workflow is broken.

Regarding the use of Excel spreadsheets, the blind spot tribal workflows may have a commonality with the aforementioned. But while the broken workflows have repetitively used spreadsheets, the blind spot workflows typically use Excel to make ad-hoc analyses. Noise, firefighting, escalations, "superman" type heroes are symptoms of blind-spot workflows. Another one? Silence.

It's extremely difficult to detect. But it's in the nature of blind-spot workflows that they are not systematically, reliably triggered.

This silence usually ends in a lot of noise so you will detect it, it just might be too late to take action appropriately.

Why Do Tribal Processes Exist?

The answer to this question may have a thousand facets. But there are a few that stand out as worth noting in this context.

Smaller companies do take advantage of operating as a "tribal organization." There are few people and, in turn, close communication and transparency that suffice in place of detailed and documented workflows. Any formal, explicit structure would hinder and slow down operations. A great example of this is companies striving to maintain a start-up-like entrepreneurial culture.

However, as companies grow and become more complex, they need more structure in terms of organization, processes, roles, and systems. Even if the tribal operations work internally, as operations become more reliant on value chain partners, the innovative culture and lack of structure that might work internally proves to be a failure point in cross-enterprise collaboration. If this point to become organized more explicitly is missed, things evolve tribally.

Also, in bigger, more mature companies, things change. The business changes and new requirements, products, services, and variants of business models set in. Adjustments in corporate strategy and macro-economic conditions require the evolution of processes. These typically adapt quickly, but in a tribal way. Why? It is simply the fastest and most responsive means to address the shift in the business. This is great for relieving immediate pressure on the enterprise and unlocking value through effective firefighting, but as circumstances stabilize and volume grows, new processes become routine and repetitive. That's when you must pay attention.

Technology-driven innovations may have the same effect — they create new workflows. For example, take the use of the Internet of Things (IoT). Let's say sensors signaling the whereabouts and status of equipment provide information and insights that never were available before. This creates the need for workflows to pick up and act upon these signals. Without explicit workflow design, the process will grow to be tribal. In the vacuum of tribal processes, the opportunity to redefine key decision points and put structure around how new data and digital insights should shape and orchestrate decision-making is lost.

"Work-arounds" are another famous source for tribal workflows.

Whether it's due to inflexibility of a designed workflow, missed or new business requirements, or the system not supporting functional aspects, the roots of work-arounds will become manifold.

If a work-around is not addressed and properly embedded, it grows and remains tribal. With each additional tribal work-around that evolves and persists, value erodes, adoption becomes less attainable, and transformation slips through the grasp. Tribal sabotages digital.

Independent from the root that spawned a tribal workflow, it needs attention; it needs discovery to identify it; it needs initiative and action with proximity to the practical work to understand and engineer the workflow in a purposeful and explicit way. Without this attention, initiative and action, workflows simply remain tribal.

Why Do Tribal Processes Persist?

But attention, initiative, and action to turn "tribal" into "explicit" are causing efforts, it takes time, and it takes money. To be blunt, it takes significant effort to do it properly.

The allowance to spend these efforts is either based on the general opinion and belief that the change from tribal to explicit is essential, or it needs to be justified.

> "Groundwork on process design is very unsexy to sell to the top management if you don't find a basic understanding and shared belief in the need for it. How to build a business case for process work, please?" a chief supply chain officer (CSCO) in life science expressed his frustration.

It's true. When decision-makers are not bought into the value and significance of intricate process design to turn tribal into explicit, selling it becomes much more difficult.

Often the impact of these tribal processes resides at a level of granularity that is below the surface for executive decision-makers. Operators lack visibility and knowledge to recognize the waste and missed value caused by these processes. It is all they have ever known, and it has ingrained their value and position within the organization; in short, it works for them. Moreover, operating teams most commonly lack the baseline understanding of how to measure gaps to a more desired target state. With this lack of comparable expertise and reference points, it becomes nearly impossible for those at the operational level to translate the impact of tribal processes to the language of executive decision-makers.

Even if the operators are aware of the drawbacks at the most fundamental level, they lack the data and confidence to translate those pain points to financial implications and value statements that would provide leadership with the confidence to invest in the process.

Even when the attention, initiative, and action on processes design and optimization happen, it doesn't always meet openness and willingness to change.

The intention to turn tribal into explicit will often face resistance.

Those who hold the tribal knowledge feel that once they give up their work-arounds, they will become dispensable. Their tribal knowledge, within the enterprise, has elevated them to super-hero status and ensured job security. People's suspicion to become exchangeable once the secret is disclosed ignites the fear to get rationalized and to lose the job.

Maybe they invented the work-around and have tied their self-perceived value to the company in parallel with their knowledge and know-how, and a new system that will automate creates hesitation. Whatever the reason might be, resistance to change will occur due to tribal factors that have seeped their roots into your overarching operations.

The desire to work self-determined and not become just a gearwheel, the desire to maintain value as an employee, the desire to be "the only one who knows how to do something" — these are all motivations that might create resistance, even at a subconscious level.

How to Deal with Resistance?

There are essentially three ways to deal with resistance:

1. Avoid the conflict and leave the workflow tribal

2. Manage the resistance and overcome it

3. Go the camouflage way and define the process only as deep as it doesn't "hurt" and leave leeway to practice the tribal way

The latter option is the worst.

The organization spends a lot of time and resources in a change initiative that is not brought to the end far too often, and it's often because of the third reason. In this scenario, the rubber doesn't hit the road and all efforts will be neutralized. Any project, any change or improvement initiative, that suffers from "poor adoption" is suspicious to fall into this category.

The first option is not better from a workflow improvement perspective, but at least no money and energy are wasted.

The first and the last option describe what is often observed, particularly across historically profitable organizations and industries, where the lack of constant competitive and economic pressure has created the habit of preserving the comfort zone.

The net present value for executives to push large-scale transformation and address head-on tribal ways of working is negative. The risk of success and investment is high, and the benefits are not as tangible financially. As a CSCO outlined once his "Kairos moment" about why he takes on digital transformations

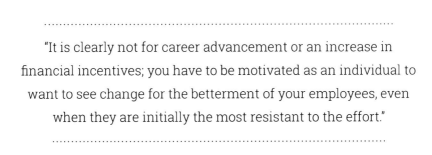

"It is clearly not for career advancement or an increase in financial incentives; you have to be motivated as an individual to want to see change for the betterment of your employees, even when they are initially the most resistant to the effort."

Coming into an organization from the outside, you can quickly detect this habit — spontaneous, knee-jerk reactions like "this does not work for us," or "we are in a highly regulated environment," maybe a bit of "others failed already with this" and, "that's a great idea, let's put this on the agenda for the future," and the all-time favorite "if only we had good enough data or skilled enough people to pursue this."

These are clear indicators of change averseness and deep-rooted comfort zones.

In fact, the second option — **managing and overcoming resistance** — is the hardest. But unfortunately, it's the only one that takes you, your workflows, and your corporation to where they need to be.

Take the challenge head on, and you'll be happy you did.

Threats, Consequences, Opportunities

There are only three scenarios where tribal workflows are beneficial:

1. The business topic is brand new

2. It does not yet require orchestration of multiple participants

3. It does not yet need to scale in terms of volume

The tipping point arrives when this business operation becomes a constant in your process landscape, it needs to be fast, efficient, effective, repeatable, stable, scalable, and open for optimization and automation. Once that tipping point is reached, tribal workflows get dangerous.

They are dangerous because they create dependencies on single individuals. As per the definition above, tribal workflows and procedures are only resident in the minds of single people or a specific group. This creates dependency on the presence and commitment of these minds — these individuals. The reliance on specific individuals also creates latency in the process and manual hand-offs to other functions, creating interchanges that are prone to errors.

If individuals quit their job, onboarding successors is typically time-consuming. A good portion of the knowledge usually gets lost and needs to be regained over time. If too many individuals leave the organization, the tribal workflow even gets completely lost and hampers the organization's ability to sustain the workflow resulting in good quality or working all.

Tribal workflows delimit efficiency.

Whatever your efficiency goals are — and most probably it's a combination of the points mentioned hereafter — tribal workflows are not sustainably taking you anywhere. You can never optimize your processes and maximize profits with tribal workflows, not even close.

Manual interaction is costly. And even if it's sometimes speedy and efficient, it has a broad variability in terms of cycle time and related efforts.

Effort impacts cost targets, while time may impact much more:

- Customer service level
- Agility and responsiveness
- Customer experience
- Inventory
- Capital employed
- Waste
- Sustainability

Tribal workflows restrict growth and scalability because they take time. **Time directly relates to performance of any kind.**

The repeatability at the level of quality required — speed, timeliness, correctness, variability — is limited by nature. The combination of dependency on single individuals, averseness to improvement, and the time it takes to complete a process all come together to impose a further risk: **tribal workflows have very limited scalability in terms of volume. Tribal workflows impede improvement.**

Innovations like new systems, process optimization, and even new hires and organizational structure changes will only improve tribal workflows partially. Why?

Because you can't digitalize workflows, nor can you automate them. **As long as workflows remain tribal, they apply a lotus effect to any improvement** — including digitalization.

Credits to Eric Kimberling and the Third Stage Consulting Group

Long story short: Tribal sabotages digital!

It's All about Habits

Digital adoption means overcoming habits. If people are involved, it will always be about habits.

Please pause for a minute. Close your eyes and try to picture your personal definition of "digital adoption."

Credits to "Geek and Poke", geek-and-poke.com

Before digging into explanations and background, we want to give you our definition upfront.

> **Digital adoption** — yes, we intentionally use this old-fashioned expression — **is adherence to** systematically enabled, technically facilitated **processes**. Digital adoption is a synonym for the level of adherence to highly digitalized or digitally supported processes and operating models, better: workflows.

I'd guess that your definition has a stronger focus on system utilization, doesn't it?

Sheer utilization of supporting systems on its own does not necessarily reflect adherence to a purposefully designed workflow.

Let's look at an industry example.

This case study is about a manufacturer with a global footprint of production networks and sales nearly everywhere. There were tens of thousands of products, global distribution, shared materials, and dependency on other internal and external sites for vertical integration — quite complex, but not uncommon for many large enterprises.

Even though the ERP landscape of this corporation was extremely scattered and inhomogeneous, they had successfully managed to organize their supply-chain planning quite end-to-end with standardized processes and functionalities, on top of a globally harmonized data platform. Visibility had helped to reduce buffers in intercompany safety stocks, lead times, and decreased inventory by more than 30 percent.

The process supporting technology was not very sophisticated, rather basic and limited compared to what's possible, but process adherence was decent.

Then a new direction was given from the top "*to make the supply chain more agile by making use of top quartile software.*"

This initiated a massive corporate program. Business case, funding, vendor selection, program setup, and the whole shebang. The program was executed successfully in a way that was amazingly and exceptionally different from other such programs we have seen. Amongst other aspects, these stood out:

⇨ The program introduced a new, more end-to-end oriented, less siloed operating model.

⇨ The program took a strong process perspective.

⇨ The program also tackled roles and responsibilities as well as the related organizational setup.

Yet, in the end, there was still a lot of Excel involved in the day-to-day work of the planners. Why?

Well — simplifying and generalizing a bit to elaborate the point — the program did not take the perspective of the newly designed roles and their workflows in its entirety. The focus was on those workflow requirements and elements that the selected system supported and missed to resolve and support other operationally critical tasks outside of their scope.

While from a program perspective, these were edge or out-of-scope cases, and from a process user perspective, these are an integral part of their day-to-day work, hence essential.

As a result, some process users saw that they were only partially supported from the perspective of their operational day-to-day process. Hence, some continued their tribal ways of working — Excel sheets and work-arounds for managing their operational day-to-day duties. Sometimes only for the non-covered edge cases, and sometimes it even resulted in bypassing the new tool.

Some adoption and system utilization KPIs were implemented early on, yet users are smart enough to sign on before starting Excel and to upload the Excel results into the new tool to use for order placement.

The general risk is that each one of these instances creates more "sources of truth" that erode the power of the integrated, non-sequential planning vision the technology generally enables.

Hence, two learnings can be drawn from this example:

1. Adoption KPIs — and to be fair this is easier said than done — need to measure the effective adoption of the operating model and the enablement of integration from a holistic role and workflow perspective, not only from the perspective of one tool.

2. There is the risk of a dangerous misperception:
   While the overall perception might be "the entire process is now digitally transformed and integrated," the truth could be "the subset of the process that is supported by system ABC is digitally transformed and integrated as far as practically adopted."

The Obvious Indicator For Tribal Work-arounds

This illustration nicely illustrates why this misperception can be very dangerous.

Credits to unknown originator; copied from LinkedIn

The troubles discussed here are not about Microsoft Excel as a tool or technology. Microsoft Excel has many applicable usages and its proven use cases are nearly endless. Although, we personally would not consider it as a central technology component in a digitalized environment, that simply is not the point here.

Excel stands here as a synonym for a local, individual, tribal element. The flexibility and "sandbox" nature of Excel empowers users to create innovative work-arounds and operate outside of the orchestration of the enterprise — it further cements reliance upon institutional knowledge. And this tribal element is typically tied to a human.

So yes, the human is the risk factor. You won't have digital adoption problems when an algorithm comes to the result of sending a control command to a machine. It will be sent, and it will be executed as long as the technical infrastructure works.

But you may have digital adoption challenges once an alert is sent to an individual who developed his or her habits to facilitate the process. So, is this a plea for mere automation straight away? No! Not at all.

We emphatically believe that people still sit at the center of innovation and digitalization. There are many areas where the "human in the loop" is needed and where automation has prerequisites, requiring it to be addressed as a journey. We'll elaborate on this in the upcoming chapters.

The Equation of Digital Effectiveness

The COO of an European electromechanical machine manufacturer said that they have almost always been successful with digital transformation initiatives. They deeply understood and designed processes before selecting and implementing technology, and they attained huge management buy-in. There was once, however, that they failed miserably with their CRM initiative. In his words, he said that this failure was due to one thing:

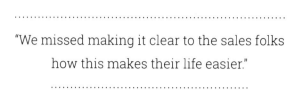

"We missed making it clear to the sales folks
how this makes their life easier."

Leveraging digital adoption means **overcoming habits**. If people are involved, it will always be about habits.

If the solution being delivered does not make your team's workflow faster and better, and if they cannot see the value, they will not adopt and go back to old habits. It is a tale as old as time.

To ensure you are addressing the needs of the user community in a way that the new desired habits bring excitement, you must pull up your sleeves, take the time to understand the as-is current state, and design the to-be future state on the level where the working processes occur.

This simple equation provides clarity on how essential digital adoption, the adherence to highly digitalized or digitally supported workflows, really is:

Digital Effectiveness = Digital Enablement x Digital Adoption

Throwing technology at vaguely or incompletely designed processes will not bring you anywhere on the journey toward digital transformation.

Digital adoption is key; hence workflows are key!

God is in the Details

You will never detect tribal branches from 30,000 feet flight altitude.

The presence of tribal processes alone is not the root cause of poor adoption. Any digital transformation initiative should consider it as given that tribal workflows exist in the organization's operations.

In fact, if tribal processes did not exist, the value to systematizing processes and workflows and driving greater standardization would be muted. As such, grassroots acknowledgement of the need to define new ways of working and support for the transformation project would be absent.

Most companies start their digitally enabled transformation journey with a common understanding: Yes, there is a better way to operate.

Our business will suffer if we do not improve the ways of working by making use of digital tools, driving efficiency, and increasing the maturity of processes consistently. As an essential prerequisite, a proper and appropriately deep as-is analysis is required. Consequently, if tribal ways of working continue to exist, the real root cause lies in the as-is analysis.

....

The CEO of a large, global system provider for
IT and power infrastructure said,
"To uncover and map processes end-to-end and to re-design these is not trivial. Preparing the grounds for digitalization means back-breaking work. It requires a hell lot of time and effort!"

....

A focused as-is analysis married with a targeted understanding of critical pain points can unveil use cases that are not systemically enabled. It allows leaders to place intention and focus on fit-gap analysis against leading industry best practices.

This is an invaluable practice, and it's what could very well differentiate your organization from the rest. It is all **about gaining a comprehensive, cross functional understanding of operations for the sake of applicable process reengineering**.

When you understand operations on a granular level, it becomes clear what's missing in order to alleviate inefficiencies. It also allows for a process-led implementation, one that finds best-fit technologies that will optimize a company's unique workflows. Not the other way around.

This is a tangible difference from standard documented, detailed as-is process flows, resulting from expensive consulting work, but pointless for the purpose, unused and not worth the paper.

On the other hand, tribal ways are always symptomatic of poor adoption. They indicate gaps in the to-be design or mere resistance.

It is not so easy to distinguish between relevant gaps and resistance since the latter is usually not shown and communicated openly, but hidden behind functional justification, gaps, and missed requirements.

You will never break resistance by continuously running after pseudo requirements. Your ability to unlock initial value will never be realized chasing countless corner cases and exceptions to the rule.

Digital enablement does not mean elimination of exception processes and human intervention. Rather, it is aiming to support these.

Just as stale food and bad news do not get better with age, you as a leader or enterprise will neither heal real functional gaps by ignoring them nor by avoiding the confrontation that accompanies the discussion of operating differently. So, this is a very thin line to walk.

How much as-is is needed if the future state might be radically different?

There is a big difference between digital transformation and classical process optimization. This will be deeper explored at a later point, but the difference, in a nutshell, is incremental improvement and refinement versus radical re-engineering and redesign making use of digital enablement.

Well, if the ambition of digital transformation is to redesign radically, how is this compatible with the statement above that deep as-is analysis is required?

As-is analysis does not necessarily mean a detailed mapping of the scoped workflows. For a redesign, you need to capture all purposes that a process serves today in a comprehensive way. Some of these processes are obvious and explicit, many of them are hidden and tribal, and they only grow their roots deeper into operations as such over time — an information feed into another process here, a bespoke report for department ABC there, a logical tweak to deal with aspects that the explicit process ignored or that grew up later and never got integrated seemingly everywhere.

> You will never detect these tribal branches and facets from stakeholder interviews, documentations or 30,000 feet flight altitude. **The magic word** for this **is Gemba**.

> ....
>
> Once again, the above-mentioned CEO —
> "Lived processes are always very different from documented processes!"
> ....

The purpose of this comprehensive as-is capture is not to consider everything and anything in the redesign. Not every aspect of the as-is represents by nature a requirement for the to-be. Aspects can be, sometimes should be, eliminated on purpose.

Eliminating as-is aspects also is considered a redesign so long as the consequences are thought through. If, for example, a tribal information feed is stopped without considering and managing the consequences on the receiving side, this will create friction. And it has a good likelihood that this information feed gets re-established.

Tribally of course.

Ignoring, or — as a more project-management-like expression for the conscious and intended way of ignoring — "de-scoping" is not an option if digital effectiveness is your North Star. That does not mean that any project must broil the proverbial ocean.

Rather, it focuses on intentional and documented understanding of the workflows and processes that will be postponed for deployment at a later date. Capturing this not only helps address resistance and eliminates blind spots or failure points later on but it also most critically enables continued motivation and engagement of the people experiencing this transformation. Their voice and their input have been heard, registered, and considered. You have removed a battleground of resistance and have a higher success rate of digital adoption.

But the "parking lot" must not be the fig leaf for cancellation.

The necessity for detail is similar on the to-be side. Radical redesign may raise a different impression. Even though it sounds more like a visionary big picture or a conceptual outline, the opposite is needed, too.

The big picture and a conceptual outline are important as a starting point to develop a to-be future state, but not more than that. To-be design needs to be highly detailed and should anticipate how the work is supposed to flow. In short, the concept must be complemented with an understanding and consideration for operationalization of the workflow.

Let's use the analogy to material flow design again.

Let's assume you were to design a multistep assembly process where components are purposefully put together to build a product. **Any movement, any turn, any tool should be designed and fine-tuned.** Nobody would ever create a high-level design that sounds like this:

"Let's inject some components, and after five steps we'll have the packaged finished goods."

That's not sufficient. Yet, from our experience, many "to-be designs" or "process blueprints" for information processes come across as just that — vague and indirect, leaving a lot of room for interpretation (aka, an open door for tribal workflows).

> Would anyone be surprised about inferior quality or poor performance of the assembly process with just high-level design? Of course not. But why do we expect this to be different with information or decision processes? That is quite naive, isn't it?

The introduction of new, digitally enabled processes requires a greater degree of explicit design and translation to the people who are at the heart of transforming the strategic vision into company value. If you expect the team to execute the vision, you must **exactly** design how this operationalization is supposed to work.

> The conclusion is straightforward: the **effectiveness** of digital transformation depends on the **avoidance of tribal ways of working.**

Detection and prevention of tribal workflows need detail, need proximity to real life. It needs pulling up the sleeves and getting the hands dirty. Back-breaking work, as they call it.

Hammer and Champy expressed it this way — "Playing tycoon might be more exciting for senior managers than dirtying their hand in the mundane details of operations, but it's not more important. God . . . is in the details."[9]

One of the amazing interviews was with the chief supply chain officer (CSCO) of a multinational life science corporation. His interpretation of "digital transformation" is deeply rooted in the assumption that the "Amazon-effect" will find its way into B2B businesses sooner rather than later.

---

9   Reengineering the Corporation: A Manifesto for Business Revolution, Hammer, M. and Champy, J., Harper Collins, New York, 1993

"In a few years from now, we must be able to act as partners in a digital ecosystem with Amazon, Google and Co. That enforces decision-making ability within seconds.
That does not work if my existing processes continue to work tribally on Excel in the end."

Detailed process work might be back-breaking, but tribal workflows jeopardizing your digital effectiveness become neck-breaking when you let it go on unchecked.

Tribal sabotages digital.

This CSCO also expressed his frustration in saying,
"Topics like data quality improvement or process work are very unsexy. What the hell is the business case for fixing messy data or detailed process work? I always run into resistance that I can only overcome when something explodes."

This is a great assist to change gears and start taking a deeper look into typical pitfalls for adopted, effective digital transformation.

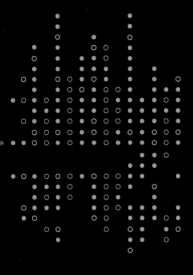

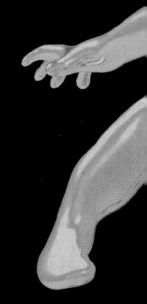

Part II

Poor Adoption Starts Early

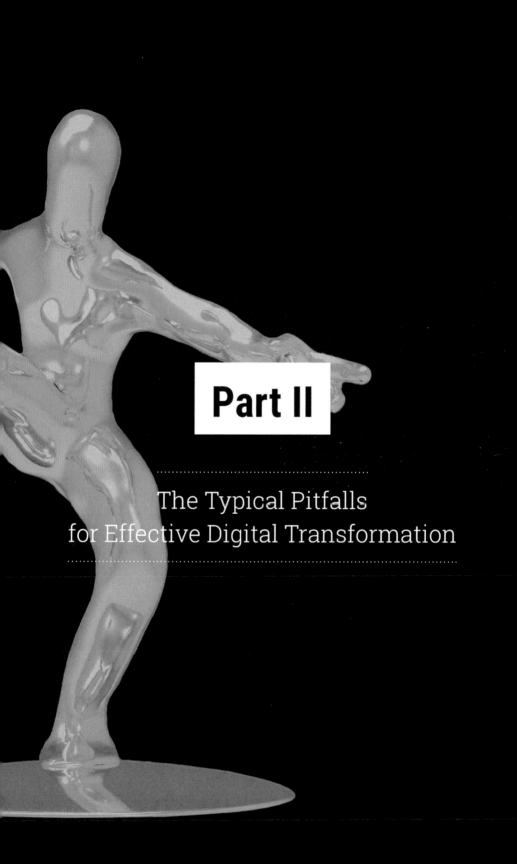

Part II

The Typical Pitfalls
for Effective Digital Transformation

Poor Adoption Starts Early

Ignite with the right ambition and spin — or leave it!

The potential pitfalls for effective digital transformation are abundant.

The selection of the pitfalls we decided to address here is kind of arbitrary and is not supposed to be exhaustive. Rather, we aim to highlight aspects that we've seen reappear again and again, and that we also heard in the interviews we conducted.

Not all of these aspects are wrong and misleading by default. In case they get applied intentionally with conscious and careful balance of their impact, it might work and not be a pitfall, after all.

But our experience confirms that many of these aspects result from a general mindset and are more paradigmatic. Without awareness of the risks or without consciousness of collateral effects, they become dangerous and lead into failure of varying magnitude. And typically, you do not just observe one of the aspects, but several in combination.

To whom does this chapter concern most?

The importance goes top down.

Those who initiate, influence, sponsor, mentor, and lead digital transformation initiatives need to question their actions and probably challenge aspects of their resident approach toward digital transformation, even their mindset. **Specifically, C-level leaders** due to their influence, budget- and ROI-perspective, and general responsibility of the company's success. Giving the right or wrong spin is costly and likely detrimental for the company. While it's fairly easy to take influence top down, it's quite hard to fix the wrong understanding at the top with a bottom-up approach.

Some leaders come into an organization, whether tenured or not, and decide that technology is the answer to solving an organization's operational deficiencies. They make the mistake of thinking a shiny new software is the silver bullet that will optimize workflows.

There are two imperative understandings that leaders need to realize as being essential for successful digital business process transformation.

1. Ignite!

Don't expect digital transformation to be a natural, evolutionary development that time will bring. Transformation needs your ignition!

2. Ignite With The Right Ambition And Spin — Or Leave It!

Once you consider igniting, either do it right or don't do it at all. The approach for sustainable, adopted, effective change needs to be much more than passing a few test-scripts and acceptance stage gates and ticking the "project successfully done" box.

> It will be a long battle, it will take a lot of energy and endurance, **it's an endeavor that takes courage**.

But since many leaders either reside in the comfort zone of their "net present value of doing nothing" or take a "classical" approach, **you've got the opportunity of belonging to the few who get it right**.

Your Kairos.

#1 — Missing Vision

Why should your organization — or a significant subset of it — reinvent itself?

Why should leaders and managers put the established power structure at risk?

Why should employees be open to supporting a process change where their established habits will be challenged, ways of working reengineered, and jobs potentially replaced with technology forcing them to heavily re-skill?

Why should anyone leave their comfort zone?

In short, company transformation carries with it a negative net present value at the individual level for most people, especially on the surface. These programs, when the vision is correct, should be empowering at the individual level and drive improved quality of life. However, on the surface this vision is lost in thoughts of automation, efficiency, cost reduction and above all — change.

In one of the interviews, a global head of digitalization for a leader in wood-processing said,

"Our business is very profitable. No burning platform resulting from there. Neither any driving force from the nature of our competitive environment so far. No need is created by the management. Hence digitalization ambition is reduced to some transactional aspects in procurement and invoicing."

The "why" behind the questions you just read through sit in one thing: **a vision for the future**.

The purpose of a vision statement that initiates and guides a transformation as a North Star is to explain the "Why?" question in a crisp and comprehensible way. The vision must be concise and digestible **across all levels of the enterprise** and most critically tie back to the benefits to employees, customers, or the broader society.

Whether the vision results from a current, obvious problem with pressure to act that creates a burning platform, or board-level pressure for immediate and fundamental change, or if it is envisioned change to address looming challenges in the market and dynamics within the competitive environment, or even if it is general technological innovation that disrupts your products, offerings or industries, distilling the *it* into a vision statement is crucial and will directly impact the momentum that a transformational journey will gain.

The vision does not have to — even should not — explain the how. What it should address is the ambition in terms of strategic objectives and the impact the initiative will have in delivering competitive differentiation for the company. Some of the strongest vision statements then go one step further, connecting the mission statement or core values of the company.

Here's another example from the interviews we facilitated in our research. In this scenario, the global transformation lead was suffering from a missing vision.

> "There was no vision other than 'We must digitally integrate!' For the organization, there was no burning platform to move until an operational problem occurred and logistics execution was nearly stalled. This helped to set the logistics functions in motion toward change, but all the other processes were still relying on Excel."

There is a common trap that many fall into when it comes to crafting a strong vision statement that fuels their digital transformation.

Leaders tend to over-engineer the entire process.

In an effort to make it "speak" to everybody, the message gets diluted. Alternatively, to explain the vision, the wow-effect gets lost over including too many words. To avoid this, **keep it simple and poignant**.

One industry leader of a leading beverage company, at the onset of her end-to-end digitalization of supply chain planning and execution stated it beautifully,

> "Our products create moments for people and families,
> if we do not change our operations those moments will be lost.
> As a leader, my job is to prepare you to be successful far beyond
> your role or this beautiful campus, learning the capabilities and
> then operating in a digitally enabled planning system
> sets you up for the future."

It was simple. No talk of financials, no mention of systems, inventory optimization or features and functions, just two messages:

1. The people we serve and love need us to be better.
2. You need this experience to grow.

The collateral damage of this pitfall — failure to define a guiding vision or a vision that jumps too short — can't be overestimated.

Without a vision, you don't lose people on the journey, you don't even have the opportunity to take them with you.

Pitfall #2 — Saying, but Not Doing End-to-End and Cross-Silo

The big improvement potential is no longer in the existing processes, but between the processes.

How often did we hear this and nodded, how often did we say this ourselves? The bottleneck is not the basic insight, but the acknowledgement and acceptance of the consequences.

The organizational structure and hierarchy of a corporation is the reflection of functions, locations, and business segments or all other given organizational dimensions.

Innovation impulses from inside the organization — often driven by needs of a specific function due to pain points or identified capability gaps — emerge from these local subsets of the organization. Consequently, it is often from this origin, often functional and local perspective, that requirements get defined, approaches evaluated, business case outlined, and budgets requested.

The organizational silos, create, define, shape, and own the project. It becomes "that team's project" and "that functions budget" from the moment of budgetary approval.

On the contrary, when it comes to digital transformation, the perspective goes beyond "that team's project" and incorporates the impact on other workflows either up- or downstream. For that reason, we strive for an end-to-end integration of processes; we want to cross borders of silos — may it be functions, departments, systems, and external business partners upstream and downstream.

The most common and desired goals of digital transformations are integrated workflows, collaboration, a single source of truth, efficient workflow orchestration, and activity automation, consolidation and/or elimination. Functionally scoped projects, projects within the boundaries of a silo, are inherently in conflict with these goals.

> Conclusively, this means we are seeking no less than a full paradigm shift toward an enterprise-wide collaboration.

The boundaries of designing an optimized operating model are no longer the existing dimensions and borders of the given organizational structure but the value stream, the enterprise in its entirety.

In fact, many of these "boundaries" were defined and further engrained by legacy technology or lack of technical capabilities. Applications were historically ill equipped to support the functional requirements across multiple teams and the digital bridge to connect disparate systems was lacking.

Much of the hype, and, truthfully, the value of technology innovations, rest on solving these legacy shortcomings. So, if that is the promise of digital innovation, the paradigm of enterprise-wide orchestration and integrated workflows sits at the core of value unlocking.

Supply chain is always a quite tangible example.

Imagine an enterprise with external suppliers for raw materials, several manufacturing plants that produce various components, others that assemble finished goods, central warehouses where these finished goods get shipped to, distribution of goods to regional warehouses, and then finally, distribution to customers. Keep in mind, that is only the forward supply chain network, not to mention the after-sales, returns and circular supply chain network nodes.

Traditionally, the management of the supply chain was segregated, for example, by location and by function. In that scenario, production planners in each manufacturing site and procurement people across the organization, finished good planners in the warehouses, demand planners aligned to regions, markets, or business units, so forth and so on.

In an end-to-end organized setup with data and visibility throughout the entire value chain, the former organizational dimensions become irrelevant. Many segregated roles with collaboration interfaces will most likely collapse into more value stream, end-to-end oriented roles.

This questions the given organizational structure and hierarchy, which also will collapse to an extent. With the collapsing of the organizational structure and roles, the hard and soft skills that are required to be effective in the new model are redefined as the demands become greater for analytic prowess, technology savvy, and business acumen.

These new roles must be competent and empowered to drive timely decisions. This will shift the balance of power for operational decision-making from hierarchical roles to operational roles, and it will consequently redesign the organization.

This is what we implicitly say when we use words like end-to-end or cross-silo to describe the new operating model.

If that is truly the goal of digital transformation, which we believe it is, then one must ask themselves — is there a pathway to success without a paradigm shift to an enterprise level operating model? The challenge we put forth is that there is not a path, at least not a success-promising path, and certainly not a path that will unlock the achievable level of disruptive improvement without this paradigm shift.

Setting up the transformational program to achieve this enterprise-wide orchestration but confined inside the given organizational structure is setting up for failure from the onset.

There are three success factors to avoid this pitfall.

1. Expose the transformation to true strategic objectives that impact the competitive differentiation and required capabilities across the enterprise to become achievable.

2. Setup a program organization beyond given hierarchies. Pull the main contributors, these A-team players, out of the operational line organization and from their day-to-day jobs. Direct them from working "in the business" to working "on the business".

3. Empower this team to invent a new operating model and to think it through into all dimensions consequently — including organization and rescaling of resources.

End-to-end and cross-silo as the true goal of digital business process transformation requires a 90-degree turn or perspective, from vertical to horizontal.

Pitfall #3 — Vertical Scope

There is a general tendency to not define the scope holistically enough by thinking too vertical and not horizontal.

What do we mean by vertical and horizontal thinking? Let's break it down.

Vertical

With vertical thinking, we mean taking a more traditional focus on a specific business function, typically related to the functional scope of a system or software category. As an example, demand planning in supply chain or trade promotions in sales and commercial or record-to-report in Finance & Accounting. These are pillars or functions within a broader operation.

Horizontal

Horizontal expands to the cross-functional interconnection with other business functions to not just improve the integration and ingestion of inputs from tangential departments or functions, but to create direct impact by enabling enterprise-level, end-to-end decision-making.

Simple Litmus Test

Here are **simple litmus tests** to help you get a pulse on **whether your digitalization efforts are vertical or horizontal:**

1. Critically question whether a defined scope truly creates a positive impact on an external stakeholder, the customer, or the shareholder; question whether it directly influences the competitive differentiation or provides a new way of working that adapts to the external market or competitive pressures. Or does it only indirectly influence?

2. Evaluate the sponsors of the programs and those that passionately fought for the idea to transform, did this group include senior leaders across multiple business functions or teams?

3. Does the vision of the program contain something that you would strongly prefer your competitors did not copy? If not, is it differentiating enough?

Let's build on the example that we outlined in the previous chapter, the enterprise with an average complex supply chain network, and let's assume a possible scope being defined to transform end-to-end planning across the supply chain value stream.

This vision of end-to-end planning of the value stream is focused on producing a single, consistent plan for raw material supply, production, distribution, and inventories to meet expected customer demand.

To be fair, this scope is already much broader than many we typically see. The outlined example seems to have a horizontal scope already, and yet it does not.

Why?

The scope of the project is to produce a single overall consistent plan. This would be an input for internal recipients such as purchasing, manufacturing, and distribution. Hence, it may indirectly improve company performance since the inputs produced are of better quality and garner higher efficiency in the downstream processes.

Yet this scope does not include a direct impact.

The reality is that we have not achieved the horizontal objective until the internal consumers of this input are aligned to execute the plan and provide circular, closed-loop feedback into the parameters that generate the plan. Simply put, the scope is not horizontal enough.

For this instance of **horizontal**, we stick to Hammer and Champy's definition of *process* as *a series of activities which, taken together, produce an outcome of value to the customer,* meaning an external customer or supplier, not just the internal receiver and processor of input produced.

So, what's missing to make the scope horizontal in this example is to include the cross-functional control processes. It is **not** about including the subsequent, input-consuming processes into the scope — purchasing, manufacturing, and distribution in this example.

But what is the value of a plan as the result of a transformed process if you don't take control whether execution and reality deviate from it and why?

This, of course, is a whole new ball game regarding the complexity of cross-functional processes, breadth of visibility, and underpinning data integration. These elements are needed to ensure that the plan generated is feasible and that executional disruptions and capacity adjustments are considered as refinements of the plan going forward. Thus, the consumers of this plan must also be accountable parties as suppliers of data inputs and be activated as business data process stewards.

There are many natural reasons that drive vertical thinking and distract from horizontal thinking. Let's just list a few of these reasons. Be concerned when you hear three that sound familiar — this indicates your organization thinks too vertical.

Reasons that Drive Vertical and Distract from Horizontal Thinking.

1. Budgets are set or assigned to functions.
2. It is easier to drive approval for a project that is entirely under my control.
3. Alignment with other teams required more time.
4. Other functions have different priorities.
5. That team just doesn't understand what I need.
6. We can't tell other teams how to do their job.
7. Geographical differences make it impossible to look at this globally.
8. We really are multiple different businesses.
9. Local considerations must be provisioned for and considered.
10. Let's start small!
11. That is a great idea to do in a later phase.
12. We are not at a maturity standpoint to do this yet.
13. Our data quality will prevent a broader vision of integration.

Now you may say that some of these reasons that drive vertical thinking make a lot of sense to keep a scope manageable and digestible.

When we plead for a holistic and horizontal scope here, we are referring to the entire scope of the transformational initiative, not seeing this as a program step that needs to be taken in one bite.

A scope can be split into a multi-step transformational road map, provided the vision and targeted end-state is not lost.

But for a holistically designed operating model and process architecture as well as for the underpinning technical architecture, it is essential to not do this step by step, but for a horizontally defined scope that creates impact. The architecture and target operating model need to be designed and aligned horizontally even if it is executed in vertical functional releases.

A vertical scope will bring incremental improvement, but not transformational redesign. **That's why it's a pitfall for true transformation!**

Pitfall #4 — Unguided Management Expectations

Disappointment and impatience start with expectations.

This is a life lesson that applies synergistically with digital transformation.

"If this fails, we need to explain it to someone
who has to explain it to Wall Street,"
the global head of operations for a global leader in the life
science space recently described the chain of expectations.

It is the magnitude and importance of the transformation that makes the initial calibration and ongoing management of expectations from the top down so important. Any program that is genuinely transformative by nature should be impacting corporate performance at a level of materiality that is relevant across the senior leadership team and even at the board level.

A business line CFO who was one of the global transformation managers in an accomplished transformation program at one of the world's largest food companies sat down with us for an interview.

....

They explained,
"We ran a multi-year program with top-level sponsorship. We nominated global transformation managers for each process. We started with very detailed process work with a lot of travel and onsite Gemba to understand the complexities of the as-is, and to develop and socialize the transformed to-be."

....

This sounds like well-calibrated management expectations and a good understanding of necessary involvement.

When expectations are set appropriately for everyone involved, a digital transformation project will have a much higher likelihood of success.

So, how do you do it? How can you set the right expectations?

Setting Expectations the Right Way

Expectations need to be calibrated and guided in several dimensions in a top-down approach. Start with the C-level executives and work your way down through the organization's hierarchy by setting the right expectations for each of the following elements.

- Nature of the transformational endeavor – Journey, not project
- Depth and breadth of change
- Presumable level of noise
- Necessary C-level engagement
- Strategic impact
- Timing and duration
- Savings and improvements
- Costs and investments
- Internal resourcing commitment and backfill strategy

The overall message that needs to be conveyed is simple. Transformation is not a project defined by a start and end date. Rather it must be approached and presented as if it's a journey. It will not only be a journey in the sense of a sequence of projects and a road map of activities, but also a shift to continuous learning and refinement. To some degree or another, the organization will be saying good-bye to the old and hello to the new.

The only certainty in business is change, and external changes will equally force agility and adaptiveness in the transformation journey.

Transformation is not an incremental improvement with superficial, local adjustments here and there. It goes broad and deep and will have an organizational impact. As such, the duration is continuous in nature as it must include the evolution of talent and operating models that parallel the growing maturity of the people, data, and processes.

It is very predictable that this change will create noise and friction. It needs trust and backing from the top. It needs patience and persistence.

Furthermore, the C-level needs to be engaged and demonstrate their commitment. A C-level leader's role should entail much more than budget approvals. It is showing personal investment.

> "Top management needs to push and to get involved.
> Also, as C-level, you need to get your hands dirty
> in the transformation process,"
> said the COO of a medical screening devices company.

The transformation will have a strategic impact and yield huge benefits over time, but it needs upfront investment. It does not pay off from day one.

Like any transformation, even a personal health transformation, the start of the climb is painful, and it is those that persist through the first plateau or two that see the game-changing results.

It will cost a lot of effort.

Smart people, people who may play an important role in operations today, need to be pulled out of their role and out of the current, operational line organization to leverage the transformation as part of the core team. These are the people with the knowledge and social capital to be equipped as you change evangelists.

....

"For a digital transformation to be fully transformative and sustainable it requires primary focus on business processes and digital adoption. That's why we are creating two new departments dedicated to our . . . digital foundations."
posted the Global Digital and Automation Leader Manufacturing of a Pharma giant.

....

As you dive in, don't let yourself be a worst-case CxO.

Far too often, a CxO comes back from a conference where the CxO from a technology vendor or system integrator got him or her excited about a silver-bullet solution — the one software that could be the missing link to digital happiness — the XYZ solution. The vendor likely sold the idea that this solution doesn't really need much more than a comprehensive system introduction and the transformation is done.

It's obviously nonsense. Plug your ears.

But unfortunately, many do not suspect anything. Rather, they allow nonsensical expectations to take hold.

Solutions that are led with technology fail to consider the human and operational aspects of transformation success.

Any promise to make the transformation journey quick and cheap will cost you ten times as much down the line.

Moral of the story, be **realistic** and thorough with **expectations** from the **top down**.

Pitfall #5 — The Mighty Middle

It exists. Everywhere. In any organization.

The more functional an organization is, the more tribal their processes are, the less digital integration has progressed, and the more pronounced and more dominant you'll find it. It's the Mighty Middle.

The "Mighty Middle" — how Michael calls it. Or the "Clay Layer" — how Klaus names the same phenomenon.

It's not defined by reporting structure, or by a certain hierarchical level. Neither is it their title. It's someone that could sit on any level of management. The commonality is their factual influence — it's deeply rooted and hard to uncover.

The Mighty Middle's power often sprouted on the lack of standardized processes and rudimentary digital tools, if any. They became superheroes through their ability to solve problems in this untranspar-ent, siloed, low-tech, tribal environment.

They typically have a long tenure and experience in the organization and they have learned how to navigate and how to build and cultivate relationships. It could be that they either inherited their knowledge and ways of working from the prior, equally evolved generation, or they may have led an implementation of a functional system a couple of decades ago, making them one of the lonely survivors still able to preserve the overview on how things tie together.

Powerful

This advantage makes them powerful, important, respected, and, well, mighty.

They know how to defend this position of power.

They know how and when to throw smoke candles.

They are brilliant in explaining how complicated things are and the barriers to change.

They know all the unique details that exist in their business and make them the dog and not the tail.

At an instant, they are ready to spiel corner cases and exaggerat-ed impact statements that cause hesitancy and give pause to the future vision.

In short, they have developed a cultural savvy in how to get things done, but also how to prevent change from happening. They know how to defend their position, how to secure their power. And when the threat is to change their job or to change processes, they pioneered and managed, and they have an untouchable purpose behind their ways driving them to resist any sort of change. It's hard to challenge and provides them a level of comfort and job security, in extreme cases, a sense of invincibility.

Good and bad

But not all empowered middle layers are bad. In fact, strong middles exist in entrepreneurial cultures, distributed organizations, and leading tech companies. Often, it's a symptom of strong leadership and empowered delegation. The sheer presence of the Mighty Middle is not the obstacle. An impassioned and engaged Mighty Middle finds ways to drive others to change, creatively partners to overcome objections, and most importantly surfaces challenges that the operational level that management might miss. These Mighty Middles are a large asset to a digital transformation team.

It's the reluctant and resistant Mighty Middles that you have to watch for. Even the presence of a passive Might Middle must be identified and addressed proactively with rigor and intent.

When it comes to change, they will typically position themselves in a way, so they are not perceived as change averse. Often, they will speak on behalf of the people who report to them and argue the lack of maturity or readiness of their organization in the light of the "horrendously complex" business. They will give their best to be perceived as progressors and champions for change who are just holding back to protect the rest of the organization.

And they may really believe that. In many instances, this can even be subconscious. They don't even acknowledge or recognize that they are becoming resistors or detractors to progress. It's just their reality.

> This setup creates a **paralyzing dilemma** for business process transformation if the problem doesn't get addressed upfront and head on.

Consciously or subconsciously, intentionally or unintentionally, the rootedness of the might in tribal structures creates a level of personal job security and self-value that gets inherently challenged with digital transformation. After all, digital transformation, by its very nature, attacks the tribal base. It causes the fear that role and power get marginalized.

It often needs senior management attention and engagement to manage the Mighty Middle.

··

A Chief Digital Officer (CDO) for a global telecom company shared, "Every week for forty-eight weeks, on Wednesday, I engaged the middle," while the managers shared details of the transformation in PowerPoint the middle explained it in operational terms. "It was my job to take this back to the Senior Leadership Team and Board and then remove any barriers, roadblocks or impediments raised by the middle, the users."

··

106

The risk

If individuals of the Mighty Middle remain in their role when a digital business process transformation scope includes their domain, and they are not engaged as part of the solution for change, a predictable dynamic gets initiated.

The mighty individual will try to take influence on the scope and size of the digital transformation. They will take influence on system and partner selection and will try to get a seat and a say in the steering committee. The natural interest will be to defend and preserve the current state, even sometimes out of a sense of responsibility and altruism.

They will not offend new technologies but vote for those who could only enable rather than question and revolutionize the current state. They will drive an agenda that is vertical in scope and functional in nature as that places their perspective in the strongest position of power. Granted, they are the internal expert(s) of today's operations.

A practical example comes from a global semiconductor company. It was 2020 amidst the global pandemic, and the supply of semiconductor chips became highly constrained. Demand was surging across all segments of the business from mobile to IoT to automotive to computing and networking.

Historically, the buying power of this company has basically allowed them to dictate terms to the supply base and serve the demand. With the crisis, this was no longer feasible. Consequently, a new practice of allocation had to be systematized and introduced into the company.

The practice of allocation became front and center for the CFO and even in discussions with the board and the company's investors. When interviewing the CFO on the current state of the business, he simply referred to one gentleman on the team, saying, "That's on him. He solves that for us."

Imagine the power of that one individual resulting from the fact that, when it comes to a decision, the executive team refers not to a process, not to a system, not to any data in their decision making, but rather to this unique individual. Now amplify that power in the fact that every investor and analyst on the street is most interested in those very same allocation decisions as the stock soars over forty percent in twelve months.

Imagine this individual being involved in a digital business process transformation where his principality of power is in scope.

Is he in charge, or are the leaders responsible for the future state of the company?

Pitfall #6 — Technology Focus and Buzzword Belief

The assumption that a system or any piece of technology entails the business solution is a dangerous fallacy.

You might be surprised that we talk about digitalization, but tackle technology focus as a pitfall. It's natural to think to yourself instantaneously, "how would you possibly digitalize without technology?"

Allow us to explain the common, often misunderstood, and nearly sure failure point of leading with a technology focus in transformations. As we discussed in the early pages of this book, the biggest semantic problem of digital transformation is the word *digital*. When you think *digital*, we push everything into the technology corner. This misleads us to think of digitalization as a technological challenge. With that, it's easy to operate from a paradigm that looks at information technology and systems as the solution to a problem.

Nine times out of ten, it's not technology that's the issue. The issue lies within the processes and workflows of the operations. When a digital transformation is led with technology at the forefront, a company will essentially take the same broken processes and workflows and squeeze them into a new system.

If you digitalize a crappy process, you will end up with a crappy digital process.

Equally dangerous is the notion that a system brings best practices and tells us how processes should work. If that's the approach, you are limiting the lifespan of your company because you're giving away all your differentiating factors that give you a competitive edge in your industry.

Last but certainly not least of all the risks associated with letting technology lead decisions in a digital transformation is the idea of a tool being so powerful, and the user interface (UI) so clean that users, aka your employees, will love it and use it instantly. Sure, maybe it's a more modern UI, but the essence of human behavior makes change a difficult pull to swallow without the right recourse. It will never be that easy. Making this more dangerous is the rise of technology companies, especially through COVID. In the global rush to digitalize, the criticality of operating models, process redesigns, detailed workflows, and people readiness are skipped over for the promises of features, functions, artificial intelligence (AI) and machine learning (ML), and buzzword solutions and systems.

The implicit expectation or assumption in this approach and understanding is that a business solution will automatically come with software or a piece of technology.

Software will not bring the business solution. This assumption is wrong!

The basic misconception is that a tool, or a system, provides a comprehensive solution and delivers conceptual thinking for us. Buzzwords often do not have operational practicality, but bring this misconception to perfection. "Control Tower" or "Command Center" are perfect examples that are used multidisciplinary.

Software vendors often use these classifying terms for their products, trying to suggest that it solves a specific problem, and companies simply need to buy and deploy it. By the way, this is not their fault; it is their job! **We can't expect them to do the critical thinking for us.**

The risk of these buzzwords is twofold.

1. On one hand, they are typically used without clear definition, hence intentionally leaving room for different interpretations and misunderstandings. This openness of interpretation allows everybody to leave feeling their needs, their vision, and their tribal processes will be enabled or systematized. In short, you are left with people using the same denomination for something that they neither defined for themselves nor commonly aligned.

2. If people follow this manipulation and do not question it critically, they are automatically led behind the point of understanding the topic primarily as a conceptual task and only looking for suitable tools and technology after conceptual penetration.

Software, no matter its type, **is just an enabler** for a transformative business or process concept.

A specific piece of technology may entail essential levers, vital enablers for a specific concept, yet it does not contain the concept, or the transformative approach as such. Even those solutions that stretch to contain process task flows or blueprints, stop at a level above granularity and specificity that is required to drive digital adoption.

Not to forget that a transformative approach is by far not yet a transformation. The approach needs to be translated into a comprehensive, consistent operating model: processes, workflows, activities, roles, and responsibilities. People need to be trained, often re-skilled, and convinced to adopt new ways of working. They need to be sold on why they should change their practical day-to-day.

Transformation is less about implementing enablers than applying new principles and translating them into well-orchestrated, practical action that induce new habits.

> Fancy technology and new enablers mixed with old habits will not bring you anywhere close to transformation. It often doesn't even improve anything; it only makes things worse.

In this scenario, the desired vision of the technology will inevitably conflict with the structure of tribal processes, creating frustration on all levels and leaving scorched earth in its wake.

Hence, approaching digital transformation with a technology focus — technology-led instead of process-led or business-led — is very risky. It not only has a limited probability of succeeding, but it may also put the operability of the impacted area, even the entire company, at risk of operational disruption.

Up to this point, we have viewed the technology-led focus from the perspective of misled understanding.

But we should not forget about the technology enthusiasts and evangelists. You may find these less on the general and functional management levels and more in proximity to IT departments. They will be less saturated with experienced businesspeople and more in the generation of digital natives with quick adoption of new technology tied with minimal business experience.

This innovative mindset is important in the context of digital transformation, but it needs to be embedded and counterbalanced. It's important to explore the art of the possible, to truly think outside the box, and to anticipate potential applications and effects of digital technology. In fact, equally damaging is defining new operating models without consideration of the blockages, latencies, and limitations placed on the as-is process due to technology deficiencies.

That said, the technology enthusiast that is not rooted in a future operating model and its requirements will consistently drive technology-led approaches if they run alone. The embedment into a team with counterbalancing domain expertise that is supported by business and change experience will yield both transformative concepts and habit-changing approaches. It's the yin and yang of digitalization.

Technology focus can work but be cautious!

Even though we see much more risk than opportunity in technology-focused approaches, we've seen it — consciously and carefully applied — as a successful strategy. In all these cases, the aspects of implementing the technical enabler (usually software systems) and transforming the business area were separated and approached as two subsequent steps.

This might be a smart transformation approach from a change perspective, but it requires perfect alignment and excellent expectation management, especially on the executive sponsor level. While the advantage of slower, better manageable, and digestible change is obvious, the disadvantage lies in upfront investment and postponed return.

If this disadvantage is consciously accepted, this strategy might be a favorable one in cases where the entire change at once, technology and process, could overstretch the organization and be simply too much.

With that said, the probability of digital transformation success increases manifold when processes and people are at the core of decision-making rather than technology. This enables organizations to find the best-fit solution for their unique needs rather than fitting their processes into cookie-cutter software.

> Don't lose your edge. Prioritize your processes and determine technological enablement that fits your company's operations and culture rather than a technology that your company would adapt to.

Pitfall #7 – No Appreciation for Relevant Details

Going on site, putting feet on the ground, engaging the base, and doing the Gemba is invaluable.

The surface of the earth looks flat and smooth from 30,000 feet.

Even from 10,000 feet, it's not significantly different.

You can see more details but by no means the granular perspective of the hurdles and obstacles at the level at which day-to-day operations take place with both feet on the ground.

It takes both an overview, an eye for the whole, and an eye for detail. A new operating and process model will only have a chance of being adopted if it is broken down to the level of user operations. At this stage, we often see various deficits that become pitfalls for the success of digital transformation.

There is a lack of awareness and appreciation for the criticality of understanding detailed work.

Awareness of the necessary level of deep dive and detail is not a matter of course, especially under consideration that this requires effort, time, and cost. For organizations quilted together with tribal processes, this also requires engagement of the middle and significant rigor to separate the implicit and actual from the documented ways of working.

Going on site, putting feet on the ground, engaging the base, and doing the Gemba is invaluable. It could, quite literally, make or break the level of success of a digital transformation project.

In order to do that, there needs to be awareness and belief. The return on that assurance is priceless. You just can't see and measure it immediately, but it will pay dividends in operations and cultural buy-in to the new norms.

> "The functionality didn't cover our requirements,
> but the statement of the Center of Excellence was
> *it's a global approach, it can't be changed,*"
> said the Head of SC Planning EMEA of a major
> Indian pharma company.

The push toward standardization and usage of out-of-the-box functionality is absolutely reasonable. In fact, these two steering mantras ensure the solution is sustainable long-term and that the organization can operate in a common cadence.

In this journey to cover the requirements and not stray from standardization objectives, it must be understood, communicated, and managed with great focus and intent to **make the careful distinction between value-adding and non-value-adding complexity, cut the latter, and take the first very seriously.**

> To reach adopted, effective transformation, relevant details trump focus on out-of-the-box and standardization.

It is these relevant details that, when not accounted for or uncovered, drive users back to creative, personalized ingenuity and tribal ways of working.

Another equally dangerous pitfall is judging and adjudicating process requirements through the lens of the system.

Sometimes, limited awareness and attention to relevant details is not the problem but rather the challenge arises due to a bias that's imposed through system-centric thinking. The relevance of these details and both granular and big-picture requirements get assessed and evaluated through the lens of a given system and its capabilities. This is a red flag that could throw things for a loop.

Sometimes it's not the system capabilities as the constraining factor, but the defined scope of a Statement of Work. In either case, the true needs of the targeted end users are sacrificed due to external constraints.

The enabling requirement is simply dismissed or buried.

While that may maintain project scope or confidence in the selected tool(s), it sets the road map for a failed transformation journey.

> Regardless of the causation, the effect is the same. Relevant details get pushed aside. In doing so, adoption is put in jeopardy.

The third common pitfall is about misusing the *Parking Lot.*

Practically, you cannot handle every relevant detail with the same priority and solve it instantaneously. You typically capture it, document the understanding, and put it into what we call a parking lot for later deployment. The parking lot, by nature, is intended to reflect back to the requesting party that *I empathize this topic and will not forget about this,* and as such should be an adoption facilitator.

> But too often, this parking lot is just a nicer way to ignore, or to descope, or to get annoying stuff out of the way.

This is the seed for poor adoption, new work-arounds, and the continuation of tribal ways of working.

Does your company's parking lot, your Phase X, always become Phase Never? If this rings true to you, it rings true to the team passionately arguing for their requirements as well. They won't forget it.

Pitfall #8 – Underestimating the Data Challenge

Integration uncovers poor data quality.

The interview with the CSCO who envisioned the "Amazon effect" spawned another interesting finding:

....

"Integration uncovers poor data quality."

....

When he said integration, he didn't mean technical integration but **functional integration** and contextualization.

Poor Master Data

When we raise data as a pitfall, many think of poor master data. Parameters, as they sit in the system, may have gotten their last update with the ERP implementation or upgrade that took place ten years ago.

We did a project across nine European manufacturing plants of a global healthcare producer. All plants had the same transactional system called MAS90, which was implemented in the late '80s.

We had to extract data, and one of those data elements was the item master with its parameters. What we found was that over 95 percent of the raw materials had an identical lead time: 42 days.

The reason for this was simple, yet alarming.

Some of you may remember Douglas Adams' *The Hitch Hiker's Guide to the Galaxy*, which became famous in the early '80s.[10] It was a science fiction satire which — amongst other crazy stuff — became known for the "Answer to the Ultimate Question of Life, the Universe, and Everything," calculated by an enormous supercomputer named Deep Thought.

And the answer was . . . 42.

You can probably imagine that this book was specifically famous for IT folks and nerds.

---

10 The Hitch Hiker's Guide to the Galaxy, Douglas Admas, 1979

Well, it was such a team of IT folks that apparently pre-populated the lead time parameter when setting up the MAS90 system for the nine manufacturing sites, and **it was never maintained**.

This example may sound extreme. But poor quality in master data is not uncommon. Yet it's obvious and solvable. Just do it.
If experience has taught us anything, it is the desperate need for business data process stewardship and the significant variance between demonstrated and stated parameter data.

Technical Integration

Another common type of data pitfall might mean issues regarding the **technical integration** of data.

The pitfall that comes with the technical integration of data is challenging, especially when we talk about end-to-end transformation and the necessity to build an equally broad data foundation or data dictionary.

This challenge is quite obvious and solvable. There are specific opinions and tactics that one can use in their approach to mitigate this challenge from an architectural perspective, but we'll get to that in Part III. What we are talking about here is different.

Master Data and technical integration of data are obvious challenges. The **hidden challenge** has pitfall-potential: **harmonization and contextualization end-to-end**.

Harmonization and Contextualization

The pitfall that we are referring to here is hidden, at least hidden for everyone who has not yet gained experience with bringing data from multiple sources into a consistent context as a single source of truth for an end-to-end transformed scope.

The structural harmonization and the technicalities are pieces of cake compared to the semantic harmonization needed. And not until they are structurally and semantically harmonized can one start to put them into context and see functional inconsistencies, gaps, contradictions, and deviations.

In a non integrated process setup, you have interfaces — one process producing output as input for the next.

Often, you will see manual interaction on these interfaces, such as people uploading stuff by hand. Here's also an automated interface, but some magic needs to be applied there, otherwise, people extract data to their local spreadsheets and apply tribal logic.

In short, there are many little points of interpretation, correction, and influence — a lot of tribal knowledge. Functional integration forces you to discover and fix all these data deficiencies. In this sense, "Integration uncovers poor data quality."

We often refer to this as a company's data that is "not fit for purpose" concerning the objective of unlocking enterprise and cross-functional integrated transformation.

The functionally integrated and contextualized data is the foundation of your digital transformation.

Considering that trust in this underlying data is probably the most fundamental layer of adoption, this is a serious pitfall.

Pitfall #9 — Project Mentality without Approaches to Sustain the Change

Seeing digital business process transformation as a project is like expecting the transition from a couple to a family as a simple step change with the start and end date defined by the period of pregnancy.

Calling a major transformational initiative a "project" automatically evokes certain expectations and associations.

A *project* is typically defined as a change activity that leads to a targeted result for a defined scope within an intended period and budget.

A **digital transformation** is not just a project.

In fact, it **is a journey**.

It is a new phase in life, in the example of the couple. It may sound like a platitude, but it is much more. Things will change enduringly. If you don't prepare for this, you'll be in trouble.

If you look at deployments of new ways of working, supported by new tools and technology, with respect to adoption, you can often observe a peak in performance within six months after the deployment started.

With high focus and attention, process users get ramped up regarding capabilities, comfort, and confidence. Training is reiterated for those who might not yet be fully comfortable. You measure performance and adoption, and you are likely to see KPIs increasing. Things seem to have gained solid traction.

But things are — of course — not perfect and not perfectly complete from the beginning. As process users grow into the new world, new questions and new use cases arise, and corrections and leftovers that have been put in the parking lot start to surface. These requirements are often interpreted as signals of resistance, but they are not. They are typically signals of adoption getting traction and more often than not, growing process and organizational maturity.

If you look at it as a project, your support efforts will likely fall flat due to a lack of post-go-live recourse, and your digital transformation will start to implode.

The only guaranteed constant in business is change.

An even more common reason for new questions and corrections surfacing months after deployment is that business strategies and external factors have changed.

This is a decisive moment.

Thus, if the transformation approach is not one that understands the need for constant metamorphosis to support changing strategies, economic conditions, competitive landscape, product portfolio, customer channels, and all other nuances of business operations, the fall of adoption is all but assured.

> With a journey approach, you set the sails and use the wind to get going. With a project approach, you leave the boat tied at the dock and anchor down.

The lack of ongoing support and refinement will kill the momentum. If there is a missing mindset for continuous improvement, if the program and transformation are designed as a project and not as a journey, it will act as a toxin that seeps into the organization and into the individuals who run the day-to-day operations.

Their frustration and resignation will quickly erode adoption.

Users go outside new tools and ways of working and will reapply tribal ways of working or invent work-arounds that allow them to get their work done. They will adapt in the way of their own creation rather than an intentional, strategic way set forth by leadership. They will find a way to garner a level of comfort and confidence. Thus, creating a downward spiral that gains momentum faster than you'd like it to.

The companies that are **most successful** in getting their transformation practically adopted and effective are the ones who apply a vision and **mindset of continuous improvement and adaptability**. They do not allow distraction from that path by any of the other pitfalls being described here.

Pitfall #10 – Overstraining Change Management

Classical Change Management will never compensate for the omission of missing out on detailed workflow design.

Successfully transforming a horizontal, holistic, end-to-end scope that stretches beyond a function or silo is primarily about the integration. It's about the orchestration of functions and tasks that have been scattered. They have been enabled and supported by domain specific, yet functionally appropriate technology. In addition to the technology boundaries, successful transformation requires the reintegration of multiple people and a requisite adjustment in decision process enablement and execution.

Let's translate this into a simple example.

137

Imagine that the main functions of driving a car — steering, accelerating, braking and forward visibility — are distributed into roles between four different people. To move the car, these four people need to coordinate their actions continuously.

Every steering movement, every braking action, every acceleration, and every evasive measure corresponds to a decision. Each of these decisions are enabled by the forward visibility function.

Your transformation approach is essentially the equivalent of integrating all these four functions into a single driver.

Many transformational projects we've seen put their focus on building and fueling the new, integrated car. A lot of effort is put into the design, conceptualization, implementation, testing and refinement of the car.

Since everybody knows, or at least has heard, how important "Change Management" is, they also complement the exciting approach of building a car with some classical change management means, such as:

- Shaping and communicating the vision of having a fantastic car that is faster than the competitors' ones,

- Lots of communication to prepare the people and the organization,

- Stakeholder analysis,

- Marketing the benefits to the consumers of the car's functions,

- Training concepts to familiarize the future drivers with the operator's manual to make sure they know where the switch is to turn on the headlights.

This approach misses out on two important, intertwined elements that are absolutely essential for effectiveness and adoption.

1. The construction of the car and all its functions need to be a result of a very detailed analysis and concept of where and how to use it and of the process and workflow thought through down to the level of the day-to-day operational work.

2. The drivers need to be incorporated into this process. They need to be educated and practically trained. They must be proficient in regular operating, in strategic plays, and in their reactions to disruptions. This all must be considered throughout the car design process already. While tailoring to the driver's unique nuances, the car must be designed for more than just one potential driver.

Classical change management will never compensate for the omission of missing out on detailed workflow design and driver-centricity.

Some say that change management is the cure — if the people are taken care of, then they will adopt the new technology with ease, and a digital transformation will be successful.

Sure, change management is important.

But what's more important is detailed workflow design. Your people need to know exactly what they are supposed to do in the new state of business. If there is any room for interpretation, then tribal will sabotage your digital achievements quickly.

The **workflow** and the knowledge and ability to apply is the **connecting** element between **people and technology**.

This is why we argue people are still at the heart of innovation and transformation. Assuming anything less than this is sufficient is the fallacy of historical overtraining and years of advocating the impact that superficial change management can bring.

When we step back and review failed projects, there are always three guaranteed factors.

1. A Lack of planned time for user proficiency baselining,
2. Hard- and soft-skill training,
3. Pre-launch proficiency testing.

Successful transformations never miss testing the data, the integrations, the use cases, the functional flows, and the configurations. However, nine out of ten programs never test the drivers' ownership over the capabilities or competency of maneuvering the new car.

With the assumption that a pinch of change management is sufficient, **transformation will fail.**

Pitfall #11 — Vendors and Advisors

Some unloved truths.

When it comes to larger-scale transformations, there are two typical parties at the table — technology vendors and technology advisors.

Technology and Software Vendors

Most software vendors have moved to a cloud-based offering and are driven to generate software-as-a-service (SaaS) revenue. Annual recurring revenue (ARR) became the number one metric that determines their company's valuation; therefore, it is the focus of their conduct and the main incentive of their sales force.

ARR being the focal point, removing all barriers to SaaS subscription revenue is important: deployment cost, integration complexity, user and data readiness, the need for process work, or, above all, change management cost. Making these topics look unimportant and tiny leads to a premium in shareholder value for the SaaS vendor.

Even though all these vendors try to speak transformational language and associate their software system directly with value generation, may it be an increase of margin and revenue, cost savings, customer experience, service improvement, etc., they are trying their very best to hide two interrelated facts.

1. Their system enables processes to create the value, but without these processes, their direct value-add is limited.

2. They have NO real interest in reengineering, upfront design of an operating model, deep-diving process work, organizational adaptation, change management, and all this. Why not? Two simple reasons:

   a. It costs time and postpones their point in time to sell, to book revenue, and increase ARR.

   b. It takes a portion of the budget and costs additional money, which typically does not accelerate the decision process.

To sell as big and as quickly as possible, they suggest and feed the message that the software system is already the right business solution and that, of course, all possible use cases can be mapped as required. "We can configure this to fit your needs," they say.

Depending on how early in the initiation of the transformational journey tech and software vendors get a voice and how much the general opinion and mindset are dominated by technology focus and buzzword beliefs, the transformation journey might be derailed right from the onset.

Most software vendors are not overly eager to implement themselves. Here's some simple math — while software margins are typically above eighty percent, margins of professional services rarely exceed twenty percent. So where might the attention and investment of software vendors focus?

They will picture the shiniest, most effective, and highly functioning solution, and they may even suggest functionalities that are not necessary. They would make more money this way rather than consulting you on the best plan forward.

Every dollar of software margin spent on retaining, hiring, and enabling professional services reduces the return on invested capital (ROIC). That is a dollar that can generate a four to ten times higher multiple if put into R&D.

Also, let's be honest, managing people and transformation projects is hard and messy. Managing software functionality isn't easy, but it has a lot fewer variables than people-centric change.

This fact is not only providing little counterbalance to overpromising in the sales process but also brings the second party to the table: Advisors.

Advisors

There are three different types of advisors.

1. System integrators

2. Strategy consultants

3. Technology-competent process consultants

System integrators

System integrators are typically in the pole position in case of strong system- and technology-oriented approaches. Programs that are led by IT departments will simply march out to their ERP and Application Management Services (AMS) providers. Despite the absence of relevant domain or technology proficiency, they become part of the typical three bids process and fuel the dynamics that we describe in the next pitfall we'll talk through.

For system integrators, aspects around process-design, change management, and adoption have been pushed in the background and their focus is on the point of integrating and configuring software. The advisor's competency in driving transformation is often second to the system integrator's experience with the legacy systems or historical integration track record. This entirely misses the point.

They place themselves in the slipstream of the software vendor without the ambition to really transform if not asked. System implementation is their business model and money machine. Most system integrators act as vendors' extended arm is the "vendor agnostic advisor's costume," but often they are biased and not agnostic at all.

In fact, they may have backend agreements with specific software vendors that pay a commission when their solutions are plugged into a deal. In such cases, this bias will impact their objectivity and influence the guidance they provide.

Even worse, in many cases they do not really have the specific solution knowledge in house. Rather, they will leverage sub-contractors and just burden the project with program managers and business advisors with little seasoned experience transforming operations with the selected platform.

But to be fair, with reference to the introduction to this Part II of the book, they will reliably help you to get your system implementation passing UAT scripts. They will help you; it just may not be the best help you could get.

Strategy consultants

Strategy consultants are at the opposite end of the spectrum compared to system integrators. They are often invited to the table when the understanding of the challenge is not only regarding a big system implementation but more so a comprehensive business transformation.

Comprehensive transformation means big investments that typically engage C-suite and board-level leadership. As such, their trusted allies — strategy consultants — are interjected to drive advisory services, often at a level of granularity that is foreign to their day-to-day business.

Most of the noteworthy strategy consulting firms have started to expand into the area that had been a "dirty corner" for a long while: system implementation. Yet expertise, experience, and dedication are questionable since it is simply not their domain. There is a granularity of workflow and tribal processes that must be uncovered deep in lower levels of the organizations instead of well-designed PowerPoints. Rather, the heart of an operator is required.

Their strength and origin is the *strategy*, and nobody doubts that strategic process design, probably down to level three, might be part of this.

The operationalization of a new operating model requires a deep dive and detail in both spheres, technical enablement and processes. In order to do it correctly, it should be on a level of granularity that detects and avoids tribal ways of working.

Technology-competent process consultants

Technology-competent process consultants have a characteristic that is an advantage and disadvantage at the same time — they see deep and wide into the space of digital business process transformation.

They know that technology and software systems are just enablers.

They know the importance of a new operating model, process design, workflows, and their orchestration.

They know what it takes to leverage adoption sustainably.

They know that true effort and cost are like an iceberg: only one seventh is visible, and the rest is below the waterline.

But technology-competent process consultants are also commercial firms, hence why they are interested in winning customers and doing business. Depending on the individual competition, the deep and broad knowledge can turn out as a disadvantage if applied openly and honestly.

Not everyone wants to hear the truth. Even less want to budget and resource appropriately for the harsh truth.

In the end, this individual competitive environment is set by the party who wants to transform. If the transformational ambition is sincere, this environment will be set appropriately.

Otherwise, it perfectly leads over to the next pitfall.

Pitfall #12 – Mechanisms of RFPs and Purchasing

The first item cut – CHANGE – is the epitome of the program's objective.

A Request for Proposal (RFP) is the synonym for a typical purchasing-led, competitive vendor selection process. Many potential suppliers are requested, a "beauty contest" of sorts is held, which ends with the selection of three potential contenders. Then, the battle begins.

Of course, one cannot generally lump all RFP processes together.

The actors involved, the decision-making process, the power structure, the structure of the requested content, the selected finalists – all of this is different from case to case.

There may be a dependency on the technology focus that we described earlier. The more present this is, the more we see the following dynamic.

In the first round of proposals and offerings, there will be a significant amount of conceptual work on processes, organizational design, and change management around the core software implementation and deployment elements. Depending on the homogeneity or differentness of the final RFP participants' character — see the types of advisors mentioned in the previous chapter — you will already see differences in the initial proposal. For some, the 'soft stuff' — process, people, change — is more decorative; for others it is much more central, hence carries more effort.

The requirements for the software, its implementation and deployment typically have a much more distinct and precise description than the "soft stuff". This leaves room and flexibility for different approaches, but also for a different focus and intensity.

This is where the typical dynamic begins, since a main focus — being purchasing led, commercial process — is on costs. And now, over several rounds of discussions and proposal adjustments, you will see that process work and change management will disappear or will be reduced to a cosmetic level.

The purist definition of transformation is one of material change, significant in magnitude.

The focus to manage cost, as opposed to risk mitigation and value realization, drives advisors to reduce in program and change management first.

It's ironic and a little deflating, that the first item cut — **CHANGE** — is the epitome of the program's objective.

Even if things started with true transformational ambition, these mechanisms could reduce the approach to what it was not supposed to be: a mere system implementation.

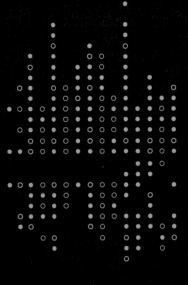

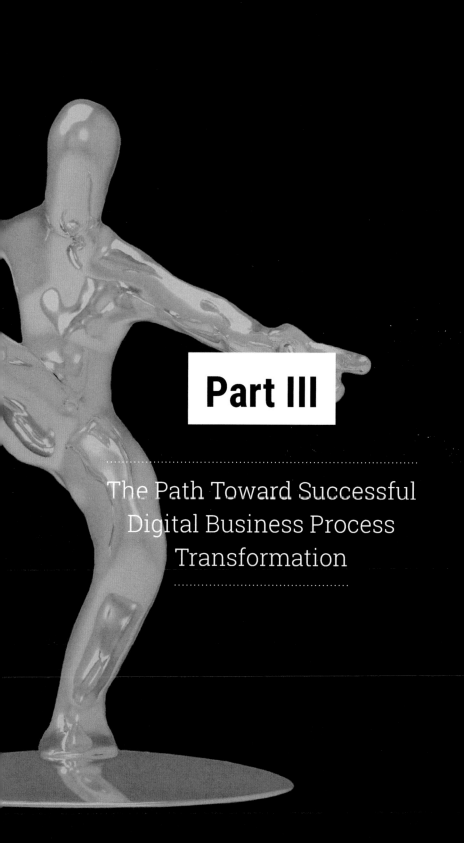

Part III

The Path Toward Successful
Digital Business Process
Transformation

Acknowledge the Differentness of Digital Transformation

Digital Business Process Transformation is process and business REENGINEERING.

Part of the challenge to achieve successful digital transformation is the acknowledgement that it's something new.

Many leaders genuinely believe they have been undergoing a digital transformation for decades. One could argue that operational leaders have been on a long journey seeking process improvements through the utilization of innovative systems and technology ever since the invention of ERP systems. So, one may question if today's "digital transformation" is just another hype cycle or buzzword of the decade, but in reality, it's actually quite historical.

While this commonly held belief may not be completely wrong, it misses the one aspect that makes digital transformation truly different:

A transformation is a metamorphosis of processes and operating models.

Lacking recognition of this critical truth sets many digital transformation journeys charted on a poor course. Digital transformation does not just build on the as-is. It does not just incrementally improve a given process within a given structure. The ambition that *transformation* implies is to rethink and re-engineer processes completely, making use of the game-changing power and potential that digital technology unfolds.

Digital Transformation is not just automating an existing process; it's not just renovating the process-supporting software; it's not just applying continuous improvement.

Digital Transformation is not just about integrating people, process, data, and technology within a vertical scope or function. It is not just about adding new, fancy analytics that serve as insights into a process that remains unaltered.

It's none of those things. I'll tell you what it is.

Digital Transformation is Process and Business Reengineering

Hammer and Champy put it like this:

> "Reengineering is about beginning again with a clean sheet of paper. It is about rejecting the conventional wisdom and received assumptions of the past. Reengineering is about inventing new approaches to process structures that bear little or no resemblance to those of previous eras.
>
> Reengineering is the search for new models of organizing work. Tradition counts for nothing. Reengineering is a new beginning."[11]

In this sense, *reengineering* and *transformation* can verily be seen as synonyms.

Defining digital transformation as a radical or disruptive and not incremental change has, of course, a significant impact on the approach required to be successful.

"If you do not begin at the end, you end at the beginning."[12]

---

11 Reengineering the Corporation: A Manifesto for Business Revolution, Hammer, M. and Champy, J., Harper Collins, New York, 1993
12 "The suitable way is backwards, but they work forward," David Ginat, Journal of Computers in Mathematics and Science Teaching, vol. 24, no. 1, 2005

In other words, start with a vision. Start with the big picture. If you don't, you run the risk of incrementally improving fragments of a given process.

That's neither wrong nor bad, and it can also yield decent results of improvement. But keep in mind that it may cement a given setup. Some improvements will have been achieved, but the need for change, the "burning platform," and the willingness for further investments fades away. In these cases, the desire to see payoff from the investment to drive incremental change stops all inertia to the transformative end state.

When this happens, *Phase 2* frequently becomes *Phase Never* as attention and focus shift. The second facet of the transformation loses energy and interest from stakeholders. The digital transformation journey then begins to lose momentum, focus, and resourcing.

On the other hand, you may miss the opportunity to change things more fundamentally, challenge principles, to think outside the box, to begin with a clean sheet of paper, as they say. According to Hammer and Champy, the "cementing effect" of incremental improvements makes the opportunity to transform harder to revitalize later.

The Relevance of a Vision

For that reason, you must begin at the end. You must start with a bigger, visionary idea to prevent the entire initiative from ending at the beginning. It's this horizontal, well-thought-out vision, that ensures momentum to build up through the entire digital transformation journey, even if this is taken in consumable steps.

The reality is that words like *vision* or *big picture* may sometimes scare people off. It may appear too big, abstract, or theoretical.

But it's not.

At least it's not meant to be. The decisive question is the one for the right reference base, the right object, the right scope for the vision. This scope does not have to be everything and anything at once; it's not the corporate vision of digitalization in its entirety.

The ideal reference base, the "object" to apply digital transformation practically, might be a certain process, a product or business area, a business function, and/or a segment with a defined purpose to provide an external or internal customer with a specific service or outcome.

Any well-defined business subset that aligns with Hammer and Champy's definition of **process** as *a set of activities that, taken together, produce a result of value to the customer.*

The "customer" in Hammer's and Champy's thoughts is **a real customer**; this is essential. It's not just the internal recipient, not just about the result that one process produces and the next internal one consumes as an input.

Let's take Supply Chain Planning as an example.

Say you define your transformational, end-to-end scope as the following:

The cross-functional process from demand planning to supply and inventory planning under consideration of capacity and material constraints.

You are most likely jumping too short.

The customer of this scope is purchasing, manufacturing, distribution, and other internal teams. They are the recipients of this change, and they will be fed a proper plan through this process. But this does not impact your real, paying, external customer unless reality adheres to the plan. Neither reality nor the input-consuming functions will ubiquitously act in union if you fail to include "Planning and Execution Control Processes," into your scope.

We'll come back to this example later.

You can easily transfer this example to financial planning as well, where you'd need to define your shareholders as the customer and even the investment community rather than just the internal departments.

What's needed as a vision, as a big picture, is a concrete, tangible description of a visionary, reengineered to-be, future state of the scoped area. The vision does not have to answer the question, "How do we do it?"

Rather, and more importantly, it should address the resulting achievement, which consumers stand to benefit, and why the transformation is holistic and disruptive enough to provide competitive differentiation once realized.

Remember the healthcare CSCO whom we quoted already with the **Amazon effect**. Let's take his vision statement as an example.

"We envision the need to act as partners in a digital ecosystem with Amazon, Google, and others on the customer and demand side. This ecosystem demands and enforces decision-making ability within seconds; hence an entirely integrated supply chain to achieve this immediate responsiveness reliably without turbulence in the downstream delivery is the only measure of success."

That's a vision; that's a big picture!

The guiding question for the visionary statement is not *how* can we improve the existing process to achieve the defined service/outcome more efficiently or more reliably.

It's more along the lines of, *what is* — under consideration of digital enablement — *a game-changing achievement*, a fundamental value-add in delivering the defined service/outcome, the positive impact to external stakeholders, and tangible competitive differentiation. In other words, what is it that will really make us different? How can we expand on our competitive edge through processes and technology?

Let's talk about another great real-life example:

There is a corporation that provides load carriers as a service, based on a circular pooling system. These load carriers are provided to manufacturers who use them to carry their products. Their products and associated load carriers get distributed to the point of consumption.

While the products get consumed, the load carrier is left over and collected. They are brought into refurbishment centers to be inspected and, in the case of damage, repaired. From there, they are to be reissued into the circuit.

The vision that this company has put in front of their digital business process transformation within one specific service segment and region is as follows:

"We want to enable White Glove Service for our customers. This stands for exceptional customer experience with minimized administrative efforts, high service level, and perfect reliability. We provide our services in a highly automated way with maximized efficiency and minimized waste by making use of digitalization. This brings value for our clients and business partners, leverages competitive advantage, and contributes to our sustainability targets."

This is a prime example of a vision to spearhead a digital transformation.

The Digital Transformation Dilemma

The approach to start at the end, to make use of game-changing digital enablement of innovation, has an **inherent dilemma**: **venturing into the unknown or even unproven.**

At the very beginning, the potentially game-changing power of digital enablement is more or less unknown, at least not yet experienced. So, it's a fair question to ask — how can you anticipate the opportunities and potential impact of digital enablement to envision a disruptively different future state?

No doubt that it needs some smart minds with good understanding of the scoped business area, visionary power, paired with imagination and/or experience in digital enablement and transformation. But it takes more than that.

Beyond identifying the North Star, you have to translate it into a plan. It's equally important for the translation of the vision into a new, digitally enabled operating model. The conceptual level of *how we manifest the vision* is at the forefront of the operating model design.

There's no magic formula on how to overcome the dilemma, but the subsequent five chapters may give some guidance.

⇨ The size of the monster, the magnitude, and nature of the challenge that digital business process transformation implies, is dependent on the characteristics of the business processes. Let's elaborate on this distinction first.

⇨ For areas with true transformational challenges, digital business process transformation is not a one-step approach. Our maturity model may give you guidance regarding the main steps and developments needed for this journey.

⇨ Even though the proper path to success is "workflow first, technology second," there is no digital transformation without innovative technical enablement. But the traditional "let's smartly select the best-fit system" does not work here. New paradigms are required to do this right.

⇨ Sparking positive momentum and leading your organization to success is much less dependent on technology and "hard facts" than on the people involved and affected. Change management designed to manage the soft factors of change purposefully is the lubricant that is essential in combination with a smart approach.

⇨ Tribal ways of working will reoccur if process management is not understood as a matter of continuous improvement. So, it's also important to look at needs and strategies to sustain a transformational achievement.

Areas of Business Process Transformation and Their Respective Challenges

Most operational and tactical decision-making processes in companies are left to the tribal state — not structured, not orchestrated.

We have spoken about processes in a quite undifferentiated way so far. But in terms of their challenges to become transformed they are as different as in terms of their status-quo.

Let's start with a provocative statement to put the finger directly into the wound.

Most operational and tactical decision-making processes in companies are left to the tribal state. They are not structured, and they are not orchestrated.

While responsiveness, agility, and resiliency are imperative for any organization in today's VUCA world (Volatility, Uncertainty, Complexity, Ambiguity), the processes that are supposed to put and keep things on track are typically the least structured or organized. We seek systemization to speed up decision-making for targeted measures, yet we lack the ability to define the course of action and the rules.

To see how digital business process transformation can help to change this, let's first take a deeper look into the characteristics of business processes as this differentiation is relevant for the nature and magnitude of the implied change and transformational challenge.

Let's make a very simple differentiation of processes with this *Process Classification Quadrant*. This four-field quadrant has two dimensions — one being process complexity, the other process explicitness.

Any of the four values — simple/complex and tribal/non-tribal — are determined by some characteristics that may occur in combination or not.

Process Classification Quadrant

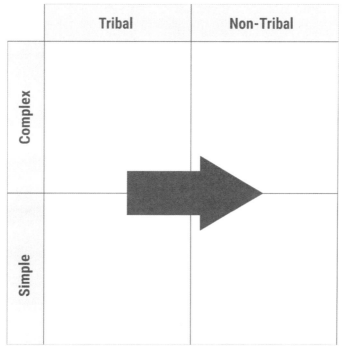

Figure 1: Process Classification Quadrant

Simple Processes

Processes of a transactional nature are defined as **simple processes**. These are processes where a defined input is turned into a defined output without the need for complex decision-making. In this context, *simple* also means little collaboration and little cross-functional interaction.

171

Typically, these processes are rather static with a low frequency of change. Also, many technical control processes — a temperature of x stops the engine — are positioned in this category as well. This is because the sequence of activities is kind of naturally determined. These processes are self-contained. For that reason, **one should seek to drive efficiency, speed, and automation in simple processes.**

Complex Processes

Whenever the sequence of activities is not naturally predetermined, and when neither the input nor the output is clearly predefined, processes are dubbed as **complex**. Decision making processes — whether operational, tactical, or strategic — are of this nature.

They typically also meet another characteristic in being collaborative across boundaries of functions, departments, locations, and business partners. With different personas and parties involved, the process typically also crosses the boundaries of systems and information pools. This is called **cross-silo**, and when these **processes tend to overstep those silo boundaries, they naturally become more complex.**

The factual complexity is usually business-driven. In a constantly changing business world, this means that such processes are subject to more frequent changes and adjustments. On the other side of the coin, we see these processes are the ones that typically drive the most business value creation. They can equally be materially detrimental to business performance. As such, **complex processes must constantly evolve with business strategy and external factors.**

Tribal Processes

With focus on the actual lived process, the central feature of tribal is that the flow — the sequence of actions and activities — is not explicitly organized and structured. **Such processes are purely knowledge based, often quite manual and not very integrated.** Personal interaction, e-mails, Excel workbooks, etc., are typical symptoms to observe.

Quite often, as discussed earlier, these have evolved over time through institutional knowledge and human ingenuity to address a need or work around a gap in the explicit processes rapidly.

Non-tribal Processes

In contrast to tribal processes, the lived working flow of non-tribal processes is explicitly organized and structured — no gaps. Whether and to what extent this is also digitally supported, integrated, or automated is neither decisive nor material in the definition of non-tribal. In any case, the explicit nature creates the basic prerequisite for non-tribal processes.

The goal is, with any digitalization effort, to turn tribal processes into non-tribal processes. To do so means improving operations. This only comes when we remove the gaps in process in the name of operational efficiency. The gaps in process are where the seeds of tribal workflows are planted. Over time, gone unchecked, they blossom.

But these are weeds that we don't want. We don't want them to blossom.

We need to remove the weeds from the root, and this comes with the evolution of simple and complex processes from tribal to non-tribal. So, what does that evolution look like?

Moving Simple Processes from Tribal to Non-Tribal

The consequences of this move are very different depending on the process complexity, especially when this move goes along with digitalization.

The transformative challenge to move simple processes from tribal to non-tribal is rather small.

Even if the flow is not explicit, it's rather simple or naturally determined. Hence, it's more about using techniques to automate manual, repetitive tasks, improving efficiency, and reducing the potential for errors.

Examples of such techniques are Robotic Process Automation (RPA) and Optical Character Recognition (OCR) for data entry automation, email automation, document or form processing automation, and other forms of automation. Again, **the value in digitalizing simple processes is speed, reduction in human error, and efficiency.**

Such efforts face a reduced change aversion as the tasks are often viewed as menial and often reduce the value one sees in the work they execute. Automating those aspects of a job is typically favored on the contributor level.

So, the mission for simple processes is to **discover and automate**. This transformation also implies change, yet the magnitude is rather low. Workflows become streamlined and either partially or completely automated, but in a quite local, manageable environment. This can often happen without touching habits of many personas and parties involved.

Moving Complex Processes from Tribal to Non-Tribal

In contrast to simple processes, the move from tribal to non-tribal is genuinely transformational for complex processes. But before explaining this, let's first take a deeper look into complex processes to further differentiate and identify where digital transformation is most relevant and why that is.

A simplified, two-dimensional differentiation framework will be utilized to characterize the landscape of complex processes.

On the horizontal axis, we take the occurrence of a process, differentiating occasional, infrequent processes versus repetitive, frequent processes.

The second axis describes the management type and the impact of processes.

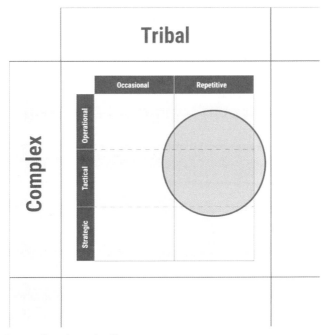

Figure 2: The Process Transformation Hotspot

Operational processes typically have executional, transactional impact, handle the day-to-day business, and describe the "doing" of the operation in question.

Tactical processes help to operationalize the strategy and to prepare the grounds for smooth operations. With that, planning, coordination, parameterization, and operational controlling have a tactical nature.

Strategic processes are about targets, giving general directions, defining rules, and taking decisions of fundamental character.

This logical decomposition helps us to pinpoint the problem area exactly where tribal ways of working hold back an organization's performance, and digital transformation is of most urgent need. These are the areas that have the potential to unlock the highest impact.

The focal point of digital transformation

Most operational and tactical decision-making processes in companies are left to the tribal state — not structured, not orchestrated. We are talking about those processes that operationalize a given strategy and prepare the grounds for the operational business by setting parameters and planning the future. These are the ones that control the plan vs operational execution vs reality to course correct and react.

These are classified as **Planning and Execution Control**. They are complex, collaborative, cross-silo, and repetitive by nature. In the way they are practically lived (and that's what counts), they are mostly left tribal.

The more collaborative and cross-silo — the more tribal.

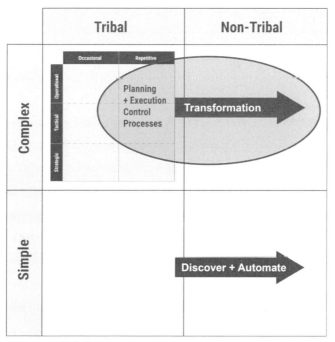

Figure 3: Process Areas and Challenges

We often see three reflexes in response to this pinpointed challenge across respected industry leaders.

1. "Oh, we've done this! We just implemented an XYZ-system."

XYZ might be an end-to-end planning system, IoT-based transportation visibility, a control tower — you name it.

So yes, you provided better visibility, a sophisticated expert system, but did you really move "Planning and Execution Control" from tribal to non-tribal? Did you touch and orchestrate the complex decision-making processes, did you structure them, or did you just support them with better tools? Usually, and unfortunately, it's the latter.

2. "So what? We've got great people — they know what they do!"

Fair point. That's great! But is this efficient enough? Do your people feel their time is valued? Are you providing your great people the tools to develop and be valuable in the ever-more digital world? Tribal processes can't be automated without making them explicit. So, how do you increase efficiency? How do you achieve higher scalability?

Technological progress will help to identify and even anticipate more and more variations and disruptions. How do you think your organization can digest this at scale and at speed while depending on single individuals and their tribal knowledge? Can you guarantee your next 100 employees will be as strong as your most seasoned 100 team members?

3. "No worries, we will apply AI (artificial intelligence) and ML (machine learning)!"

Ah, interesting. You really believe you can replace an unknown, tribal decision-making process with technology? Good luck!

The processes that we classified as **Planning and Execution Control** are a gold mine. It's challenging to really transform them due to their complexity in combination with the magnitude of change when you touch and change ways of working and collaborating. But since this lies in the nature of these processes, it's the same type of challenge for everyone.

The opportunity to master this challenge quicker and better than others, than your competitors, is enormous. These are the processes that practically leverage tactical and operational responsiveness, agility, and resiliency at scale to succeed better in the VUCA world.

Getting transformation right and sustainably effective here, at the focal point of digital business process transformation, is truthfully creating impact and competitive advantage.

It's a Journey, Not a Project — Maturity Model for Digital Business Process Transformation

The ambition to go far is important. However, an unrealistic assessment of one's own starting position is just as dangerous as the lack of knowledge about the capabilities that need to be developed.

Some things do not need a lot of explanation and professional expertise, but they're taken for granted against the background of general life experience. This includes the wisdom that things won't work if you try to take several steps at once. In life, we have to take things one step at a time.

This also applies to the digital transformation of business processes. **If you take too many steps at once, you will fall on your face.**

When we talk to people about digitalization and digital transformation, terms like *automation* and *autonomous processes* often come up, and analogies to autonomous, self-driving cars are drawn. Leaders dream of automatic, self-controlled planning, for example, or of an autonomous supply chain.

The issue here is not the ambition to go far. The issue is usually the unholy combination of two gaps.

Gap No. 1: An unrealistic assessment of one's own starting point.

In combination with

Gap No. 2: The lack of knowledge about essential capabilities and characteristics of maturity that need to be established step by step to prepare the ground for automation.

This often creates an unbridgeable gap between aspiration and reality, which leads to a classic project approach that has a high probability of failure from the outset.

To close either of the above-mentioned gaps and to avoid the consequences, we have developed the *Maturity Model for Digital Transformation of Complex Business Processes*, which we are introducing in this chapter.

We will use this model to explain the essential capabilities and characteristics of maturity, keeping the focus on complex business processes such as Planning and Execution Control Processes, but also projecting it onto Strategic-Tactical Input Processes, such as planning or parametrization.

Above all, it will help to understand why **digital transformation of business processes is a journey, not just a project.**

But before we start digging into the explanation of the Maturity Model more in depth, let's first outline an example to make it more tangible what we practically mean when we talk about Planning and Execution Control Processes and Strategic-Tactical Input Processes.

Example

Imagine a company that produces life science products.

They house a typical footprint with some manufacturing sites across the globe. They have internal supply relations where one plant produces components — active ingredients, for example — that are provided to other, regionalized plants that produce finished goods in the form of pills, liquids, powders, or other consumption mediums.

Finished goods are distributed from manufacturing to central warehouses. From there, they are distributed to local warehouses, then to distributors, or directly to large clients. External suppliers across the globe provide various raw materials, and consumables, and packaging materials to the production plants. Other third parties are used as contract manufacturers and co-packers.

To meet the customer and market demand, such complex networks need to be prepared and coordinated.

You, as a consumer, don't want them to start buying raw materials and producing when you sense that you get a headache. By the time they're able to make, distribute, and deliver the product to you, it will be too late. Hence, planning market demand and deriving production needs and material supplies for inventory is an essential **strategic-tactical input**. These inputs are necessary to prepare the grounds for smooth operations in line with strategic targets and guardrails.

The process of getting a plan consistent and continually up to date is sincerely a complex, cross-silo process that involves Sales. The sales department is likely segregated by region and/or product line and/or channel. Beyond that, you have to account for the other departments such as manufacturing, supply chain, warehousing, transportation and, last but not least, finance.

Multiple dimensions such as quantities, revenue, capacities in production, warehousing and transportation, supply, cost, cash flow, and margin need to be reflected in these processes. More importantly, the source of the underlying data, the truth of the organization, must be aligned across all teams. In an ideal state, each function or department takes ownership and business process data stewardship accountability.

Getting a consistent plan, as a result, means identifying and resolving conflicts, inconsistencies, constraints, and imbalances.

Resolving means deciding, setting priorities, making changes, and evaluating trade-offs. No doubt that this requires complex, cross-silo decision-making processes.

Many people think that the challenge of planning lies in the efficient collection of all relevant inputs and the calculations that determine the connected results.

Not even close!

The true challenge is in the resolution of these conflicts, inconsistencies, constraints, and imbalances, hence in the complex, cross-silo decision processes.

And there's a second widespread misbelief: *Execution and reality will follow the plan.*

Ha!

That will not happen without Planning and Execution Control. It's that simple.

Why? Over decades of experience and hundreds of interviews, we always arrive at the same two simple reasons.

The execution functions, such as manufacturing, purchasing, and transportation, are guided and, more critically, often incentivized by functional targets with a tendency to optimize. And that's fair, as long as the integrity of the plan is not impacted.

Even if only one function deviates, the integrity of the plan is, in fact, impacted — everything goes out of alignment since everything is interrelated.

Optimization of functional performance indicators nearly always comes at the expense of enterprise value. Why? Because most functional metrics are inherently in conflict with another function's key metrics.

It is a tale as old as time.

To prevent this from happening, or to feed back the consequences into the overall plan if it happens for good reason, you need planning- and execution-control on a tactical level.

Again, a complex decision-making process.

The second reason is simply that reality deviates from our assumptions. The market consumes more or less than planned, a production line outage messes up the plan, quality issues, delayed material supply, shortage in transportation capacity, the number of instances of variability, volatility, and deviation from plan are nearly infinite. For that reason, not only must all functions align with the plan, but they must also align with triaging and the process for course correction in execution.

Today, the interconnectedness of our world gives us enormous visibility into the physical flows, provided by real-time transportation visibility (RTTV), IoT, Industry 4.0, any kind of contextualized data, etc. This visibility is an essential enabler to knowing sooner about variations and disruptions. But it's only the **maturity** of the subsequent processes that turns "knowing sooner" into "acting faster."

These operational Planning and Execution Control processes, otherwise known as decision workflows, typically do not exist in an explicitly designed, structured form.

This is the essential gap.

Some software vendors try to put into our minds that it is just one step, just their respective system, of course, to make such decision processes autonomous. It will never be that easy. It is a fallacy that these decision workflows are not needed when technology, AI, and ML are applied.

Instead, these workflows are a key prerequisite; they are the backbone.

Otherwise, it's like saying you've built and configured a robot ready for use in a production process, even though you don't even know what is being produced and how.

So we are clear now about the challenge. But how to best approach it without falling on the face? This is the point where our Maturity Model starts.

Maturity Model for Digital Transformation of Complex Business Processes

The Maturity Model is a tool that helps to avoid the gaps mentioned at the beginning. It helps to calibrate one's own starting point, and it explains the essential capabilities and characteristics of maturity that need to be established step by step to prepare the ground for automation.

The model consists of four levels of maturity:

1. Hero Processes or Firefighting

2. Expert Processes or Visibility

3. Orchestrated Processes or Decision Orchestration

4. Automated Processes or Decision Automation

The Maturity Model is not necessarily meant to calibrate an entire organization. Different areas, functions, and even use cases may have evolved to a different level. While things like predictive machine maintenance might already be close to Level 4, other decision processes or use cases may still trigger hero-type firefighting after the fact.

Let's first look at this maturity model in the scope of Planning and Execution Control Processes.

Maturity Model in the Scope of Planning and Execution Control Processes

Level 1 | Hero Processes

The main characteristic of this level is the **dependency on individuals** who know how things are going. This is easily identified when the path to resolution often comes in the form of a name or group of people rather than a defined process.

Whether it's the "firefighter" in the disruption process or the mastermind who built the monster Excel planning sheet and supplies it with data in each planning cycle, of course, manually refined beforehand. The logic, the knowledge, and the expertise sit in the heads of single individuals.

Tribal ways of working at its best.

Level 1 is where many organizations are *firefighting*. It describes the principle to react to a problem after the fact, after it has already occurred. Now, not all firefighting is bad. In instances of the unplanned or unaccounted for, leadership with a bias to action is actually a good thing.

In times of unstructured uncertainty, the best thing to do is the right thing; the next best option is the wrong thing; the worse option is to do nothing. That said, **failure to reduce reliance on firefighting in the future is a gap for many organizations.**

Level 1
Hero Processes

"Firefighting"

Figure 4: Planning and Execution Control-Level 1

The course of action that the firefighter takes is typically not following any explicit process. Firefighting is often depending on a few individuals. By fixing one topic, it usually breaks others and causes collateral damage.

Not to forget: firefighters are often reputable heroes, sometimes acting with a senior management mandate. This is something that needs to be taken into consideration from a change management perspective. They, and their followers, will be the hardest nuts to crack.

The best firefighters are those that are most needed to be brought into the change tent as an evangelist for the vision. They have the social capital, and ideally, the respect of their peers. They must be brought into the fold. Be mindful that the transformation will inevitably remove some of their superhero status.

Going beyond Level 1 and shouting for visibility is often driven by pain and frustration, experiencing the non-scalable, non-sustainable nature of firefighting, especially in today's environment where market and customer expectations in service and experience are rising as rapidly as the number of disruptions and variations increases.

Level 2 | Expert Processes

Regarding tribal knowledge about logic and flow of work, expert processes are not significantly different compared to Level 1.

The biggest difference between Hero Processes and Expert Processes is some kind of support tool — may it be dashboards or Business Intelligence (BI) applications that provide some visibility and insight, or even a more sophisticated planning tool, as one such example.

Some tribal knowledge has been removed, and visibility might be provided to others, but most still resides in the heads of the experts, equipped with more convenient tools.

Level 2 is characterized by the fact that information is provided on incidents that are known or expected to happen, hence why this stage is called *Visibility*. By means of real time transportation visibility, use of IoT, and contextualization with other information, the events of the physical value stream are visible. The signs found in a visible state can be used for predictions and early warnings.

The biggest advantage compared to Level 1 is that **visibility enables the switch from reactive to proactive.** Even so, it does not necessarily lead to proactive variation and disruption management; it still depends on someone consuming the information and taking action.

The subsequent course of action is — similar to firefighting — not explicitly structured. What happens and who gets involved depends on the way the actors involved handle it. The process is tribal, with lots of manual interaction.

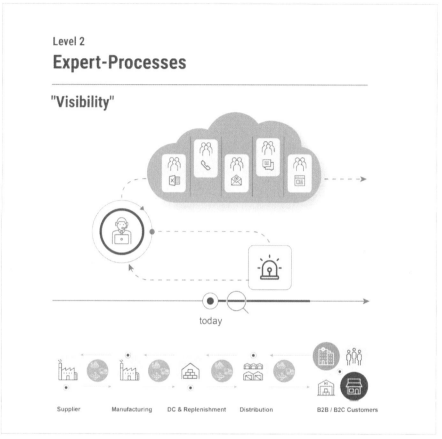

Figure 5: Planning and Execution Control-Level 2

This takes time and effort, and it typically needs a driver. Level 2 expert processes carry the risk that the time advantage of knowing sooner is lost because the process of variation and disruption management takes too long. **The reliance on human action generates latency in the resolution cycle. The time advantage expires.**

Achieving Level 2 is predominantly a technical exercise. This means applying IoT, making use of sensor signals, using a RTTV service, bringing data from different sources into a specific context, providing predefined BI reports and/or access for BI-trained users, and things like that.

This is — of course — conceptual work and implementation effort. Yet, visibility does not touch processes. It does not touch the way people work and at least it does not enforce a different, defined way of working. Therefore, Level 2 is also limited in generating leverageable results and systematically capturing and retaining value.

This visibility level is not only granting tolerance for the execution of subsequent processes but also provides tolerance to data quality. Why? Because it is consumed by humans who, by nature, interpret and evaluate the information being provided.

Level 3 | Orchestrated Processes

The qualitative difference that Level 3 brings with it is that **tribal elements are dissected, resolved, and made explicit**; they are intentionally and rigorously transferred into explicit workflows.

This affects both the process, the interaction and collaboration of a process, as well as the logic of the individual process steps. Tribal knowledge gets decoded and the flow of work gets digitally orchestrated.

Level 3 processes use visibility to trigger explicitly designed decision workflows and repetitive patterns of activities. In sports, you'd call this "plays" — everytime there is a trigger, then a play is orchestrated. This manages variations and disruptions in a structured, orchestrated, and ideally digitally integrated way; thus we call it the *Decision Orchestration* level.

The significant difference between Level 3 in comparison with Level 2 lies in the explicitness of the decision workflows, while the course of action is not explicit, but tribal in the lower stages. These decision workflows are not only supposed to be described on paper and documented for systematic enablement, but to be digitally executed in a workflow engine, facilitating the orchestration of the flow in a structured and synchronized way across all parties involved.

This is critical, and it must be orchestrated across **ALL PARTIES**.

The insights come to the process user to initiate action; the user does not have to go to the insights anymore. This is a relief in day-to-day operations.

Naturally, these decision workflows go across silos, departments, functions, and even often across enterprise borders if and where third parties are involved. But cross-silo consequently means cross system due to the different functions used in their functional domain system. For example, logistics use their transport management system (TMS), their warehouse management system (WMS), their yard management system (YMS), etc. Third parties have their own transactional systems (ERP).

Hence, digital workflow orchestration should not only target the orchestration of the people and roles but also digitally integrate the workflow across source systems.

A positive side effect of digital workflow orchestration is the reduced dependency on single individuals running processes based on their tribal knowledge. Also, the people that play a certain role for certain steps in the process do not have to have the entire knowledge across the entire workflow. This orchestration is delegated to digital support based on the designed and defined decision workflow.

The move from Level 2 to Level 3, from tribal to explicit, is the real paradigm shift. It's the start of a real digital transformation.

Designing these complex, cross-silo decision-making processes explicitly is decision engineering and decision modeling. Typically, these processes and these decision workflows do not exist, or they only exist as tribal knowledge.

Detecting and exploring them, touching them, changing them, designing them, structuring them, and everything in between is impacting behavioral ways of working. This is digital business process transformation! Uncharted waters for many organizations.

The second notable difference between Level 2 and Level 3 is the importance of data and data quality.

While in Level 2, data is offered for consumption on demand, and subsequent human interpretation can filter a lot of noise, Level 3 uses data to trigger workflows and activates people to act in a structured way. This requires data of decent quality and robust reliability. An evaluation step can be built into the workflow, including capturing evaluation results and identifying suspicions or deficiencies that can be used to improve data quality.

When we talk about decision-making, we are semantically led to the impression that it's *a decision*. But typically, it's not just one decision. Rather, it's a sequence of many little decisions, a "decision tree" that arrives at initiating action. Independent of whether this decision tree is in the head of a person or a habitual collaboration across people and parties involved. **Level 3 means making the flow and the logic explicit, digitally orchestrated, and supported in an integrated way.**

The resulting decision workflows are usually cross-functional, incorporating different aspects, views, and accountabilities into the decision. Hence, data from different functions, and different systems need to be brought into context. Some decision-supporting functionalities may already exist in functional domain systems, others need to be built and provided. But everything needs to be digitally integrated along the decision workflow as the backbone.

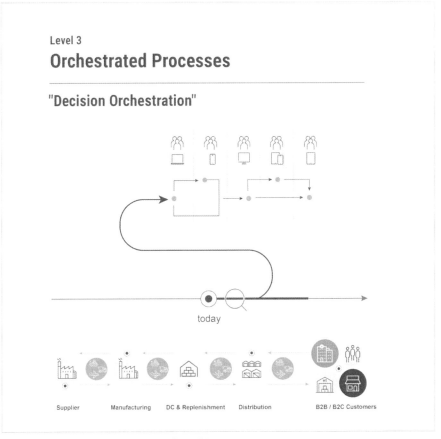

Level 3
Orchestrated Processes

"Decision Orchestration"

today

Supplier   Manufacturing   DC & Replenishment   Distribution   B2B / B2C Customers

Figure 6: Planning and Execution Control-Level 3

The interaction from one workflow step to the next should not require manual capturing of a number from one screen and typing into the next. Digital orchestration of the flow and integration of related activities is key for speed and efficiency.

This background explains why Level 3 does not only lift the bar for data quality and reliability but increases the need to bring data into a broader context. We typically refer to this as the need for data quality to be "fit for purpose" — the purpose of orchestration, timely decision-making, and cross-silo integration.

Digital workflow orchestration is not just about initiating actions based on an alert, but structuring the decision process from initiation through evaluation and impact assessment to triggering the appropriate counteraction.

Several steps might be involved in this decision workflow, many different "if — then" branches, and any step need to be supported with appropriate functionality, insights, and analytics, using the workflow as the backbone.

Level 4 | Automated Processes

Automation can now be applied to the base created by Level 3. The workflow and logic applied are explicit and are now automated step by step. **This is where smart technologies such as Artificial Intelligence (AI) and Machine Learning (ML) come into play.**

In **Level 4**, AI, ML, and optimization algorithms are applied to the relevant parts of the decision workflow. Hence this level is called *Decision Automation.*

The **"human in the loop" is reduced to** exceptions where individual assessment and decision-making are needed or explicitly desired, hence **adding value**. Interaction with systems is automated. Analytics do not only become prescriptive, but the overall level of workflow automation is increased.

Moving from Level 3 to Level 4 is different.

In fact, the progression from Level 3 to Level 4 is more of a smooth transition, an incremental improvement, while Level 1 to Level 2 and especially Level 2 to Level 3 are more, by nature, changing a principle. Hence, they are significantly harder to achieve adoption and more prone to failure as a result.

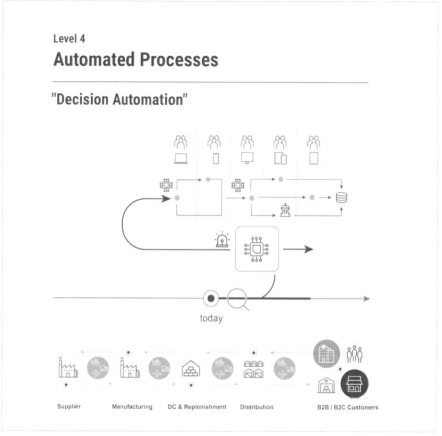

Level 4

Automated Processes

"Decision Automation"

Figure 7: Planning and Execution Control-Level 4

Level 4 applies decision intelligence to decision workflows based on AI, ML, optimization algorithms, and other forms of decision science. There are two important prerequisites for any element of the decision workflow that is taken from Level 3 to Level 4:

1. Trust in Data

It is not the reliability that is asserted by IT folks or data experts; it is about the trust that the accountable people have in the relevant data. It is the accountable person who delegates certain decisions or decisions under certain circumstances to technology, not IT folks.

2. Mature Workflow

The decision workflow has been finetuned and matured. Learnings get incorporated, and new decision cases or options are integrated. This takes some time and experience. Don't expect a first version of a workflow to be complete and perfect.

Once many events have made their individual way through the workflow, experience has been gained and captured how decisions have been taken under which circumstances.

These two prerequisites are key to applying decision intelligence to increase the level of automation in the decision flow, depending on the context of the single event.

Decision steps that intentionally remain residing with the human in the loop are supposed to be supported with more sophisticated analytics, scenario capabilities, sensitivity analyses, and decision-enablement insights.

In essence, Level 4 strives for highly prescriptive and automated Planning and Execution Control Processes, independent of whether it's the tactical or the operational side.

Now, let's briefly apply the Maturity Model to Strategic-Tactical Input Processes, such as planning or parametrization processes — to prove the principle.

Maturity Model in the Scope of Strategic-Tactical Input Processes

Level 1 | Disconnected Silos

Level 1 is characterized by the following:

- Thinking and working in silos

- Sequential progression of planning steps

- Poor technical support

- Typically, an essential dependency on spreadsheet tools like Excel

- Local database applications

- Unsystematic, not integrated, and the absence of "Control & Decide" mechanisms

The latter are ad hoc, gut feeling based, neither data driven nor systematic. The logic and the knowledge are in the head of single individuals.

"Tribal" at its best.

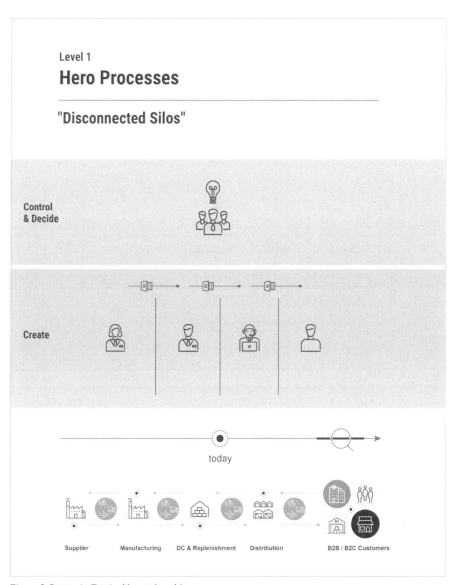

Figure 8: Strategic-Tactical Input-Level 1

Level 2 | Connected Silos

Level 2 advances by better, more integrated technical support.

The siloed process as such typically does not get transformed but is only made more efficient regarding the collection of all relevant inputs and the calculations that determine the connected results.

Neither does the "Control & Decide" side get a lot of focus.

Better than Level 1, undoubtedly, but by far not where it needs to be to achieve speed, scalability, effectiveness, and efficiency cross-silo.

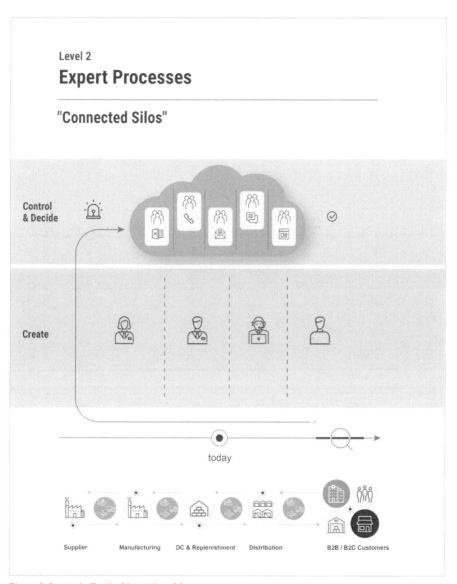

Figure 9: Strategic-Tactical Input-Level 2

Level 3 | Horizontally Integrated + Orchestrated

Level 3 is where "digital business process transformation" starts.

The functional, siloed structure gets challenged to be converted into a horizontally integrated setup. Less organizational interfaces, more integrated accountability, and more resolution of contradicting targets toward global optimum instead of functional.

"Control & Decide" mechanisms are explicitly designed and digitally orchestrated. Tribal knowledge gets decoded, the flow of work gets digitally orchestrated, and decision-making becomes data driven.

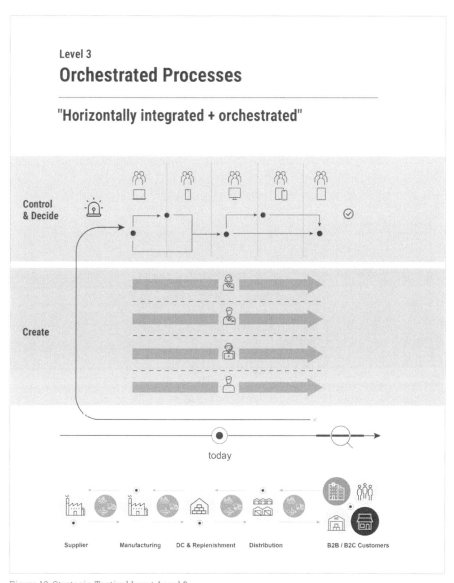

Figure 10: Strategic-Tactical Input-Level 3

Level 4 | Horizontally integrated + automated

The principle is identical: Level 3, with its explicitness of logic and flow, builds the ground to automate and focus the human in the loop to value-adding tasks stepwise. This applies to both aspects — the "Create" processes as well as the "Control & Decide'" processes.

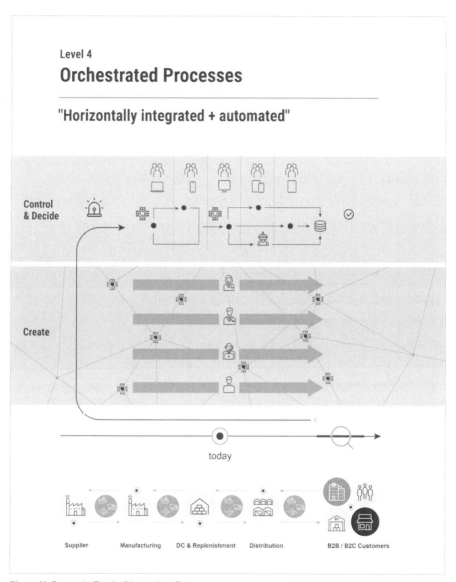

Figure 11: Strategic-Tactical Input-Level 4

Target Criteria

Let's reflect on the target criteria that the digital transformation of processes is supposed to yield and how these relate to the four maturity levels.

While *automated* or *autonomous* describe the target state in a nutshell, they are not differentiated and comprehensive enough on their own. Here are five target criteria that, when combined, effectively describe the quality of your Planning and Execution Control Processes.

1. Speed

Responsiveness and agility are directly related to the time that a process takes to yield results.

This should not only consider the throughput time of a process itself once started. The throughput time should be measured from the moment when the triggering event for the process could be detected or anticipated, ending with the final resolution.

2. Scalability

This refers to the ability to handle an increasing number of events without a negative impact on the other target criteria.

Scalability measures the capability of a process to turn an increasing number of events into decisions and actions.

Let's take transportation visibility as an example. By means of industry 4.0, IoT sensors, etc., along with increasing capabilities to use this data in combination with AI and ML to predict variations and disruptions, an organization gets a massively increasing volume of information about the physical flow of goods, delayed supplies, or customer shipments.

Scalability describes the ability to deal with fluctuating, increasing volume of incidents without negatively impacting the other target criteria.

3. Effectiveness

This refers to the quality of the results that a Planning and Execution Control Process yields in a repetitive, duplicatable way.

These are typically the KPIs that the respective process can directly influence, may it be inventory turns, capital employed, delivery performance, customer NPS, etc.

4. Efficiency

It's — of course — about cost.

On the one hand, it's about the costs that the process consumes. Not only, but predominantly, labor efforts.

On the other hand, it's the cost that is impacted by the process, such as transportation costs as an example. This is closely tied to speed as resolution options typically become fewer and as time progresses and more costly.

Efficiency should be measured holistically, not only considering the process cost as such.

5. Accountability

Planning and Execution Control Processes are complex and cross-silo. Their digital transformation needs to respect the accountability of process stakeholders and not invalidate it. Also, technology-supported decision-making must align with accountability.

Automation has to be seen as **delegation to technology**.

The Maturity Model Value Map

Let's now map these target criteria with the four levels of the Maturity Model.

The following diagram shows the positive effect of the development, and the transformation to Level 4 on speed, scalability, effectiveness, and efficiency:

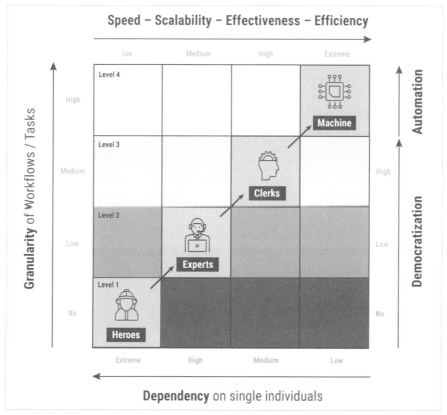

Figure 12: The Maturity Model Value Map

The decoding of tribal knowledge regarding logic and flow and the translation into explicit workflows is the key to success. Only this enables the reduction of dependency on single individuals, democratization, and use of lower-skilled labor, finally, automation.

> This may appear like little appreciation for the human in the play. That is not our intention. Allow us to repeat our belief that the heart of innovation and transformation is PEOPLE!
>
> Yet, we should not sweep the fact under the carpet that in the end, less people with different skills will be required.
>
> It might be worth a book on its own to reflect on the consequences for the society, and what social systems may look like in future, but this extravagates the focus of this book.

There's one target aspect missing in the above effect diagram: **Accountability**.

The aforementioned target said *digital transformation needs to respect the accountability of process stakeholders, and not invalidate it.*

With the cross-silo workflows becoming the central backbone of the transformation journey, the integrity of accountability can be ensured.

Automation can be applied as **delegation to technology**, under the authority of the accountable person or function. It's not the IT folks, not the technology experts, nor data scientists who should decide about automation if you want to keep accountability integer.

As a summary, in a nutshell, the maturity model teaches us that **Process Orchestration is key** to adopted, effective process transformation and automation.

The next exciting question is about the technology side of the equation — how can you best enable the process-centric journey toward Level 4?

The Technology Side of the Equation — Calling New Paradigms

Acknowledge PROCESS as the new end-to-end integration backbone and DATA as its foundation. This is the new true North for enabling technology architecture.

Even though we emphatically believe successful digital transformation originates with the theory of workflow first and technology second, digital business process transformation does not reveal its full power and value without digital enablement, without technology.

So, let's take a deeper look into the critical component of digital enablement — into the role that technology plays in the transformation of processes or any well-scoped, segmented area of your business.

Allow us to start quite provocatively in breaking with a fundamental paradigm right away. It will not be the only paradigm that we are questioning in this chapter, but it's a central one.

**Forget about a system as the backbone
to integrate and digitally transform your scope.**

If one system can cover your scope, you can be assured that your scope for digital transformation is too short-sighted, too vertical, and not horizontal or holistic enough. It will inevitably lead to system implementation, not transformation. You may realize innovation at the end, but not true transformation.

**The primary integration backbone for digitally transformed business
setups consists of two components:**

DATA

and

PROCESS,
broken down to the level of executable workflows.

Let's first talk about the "right scope" again because that's what a technological architecture must be designed for. Let's apply what's been stated in the conversations around the differentness of digital transformations and the pitfalls of a vertical scope to the scene that we've set to explain the maturity model.

Let's assume a company identifies they plan and operate in disconnected silos. It's irrelevant here whether this is supply chain planning, financial planning, sales and commercial planning, or really anything else. They are confirmed at Level 1 hero processes.

Internally, the idea of "let's digitally transform" quickly gains momentum due to the excitement of potential. This is the decisive moment that is frequently missed and almost always underappreciated.

The default focus is on the "Create" processes.

The Usual Reflex

The usual reflex for most companies is, "let's start a vendor selection process and choose the best system for it."

This should not come as a surprise. This process allows multiple partners, such as procurement and IT, to engage immediately. It typically also aligns with the power of the budget for digital programs, which often resides outside of the business function. The path is one of familiarity and has been rinsed and repeated for decades. Despite its longevity, this reflex is wrong.

The Right Reflex

Let's take a holistic view of the entire process — "Create" as well as "Control & Decide" — in depth. Let's first understand all elements, including planning and execution control, parameterization, reporting, and interfaces to neighboring processes. A planning system will obviously be one component of the bigger picture, but the architecture needs to serve the bigger picture, not just one fragment.

Let's understand the upstream and downstream tangential processes, the procedural, the data inputs and, equally as critical, feedback or information closed-loop cycles required to engage in cross-silo orchestration.

In essence, digital business process transformation is about moving a holistically defined scope to Level 4, not just one functional aspect. Any holistic scope contains multiple, umpteen different use cases with various requirements to be functionally supported. Some already exist and others don't. They will require different technologies — there's no silver bullet.

While ensuring the right technology enablement supports each function or pillar of the enterprise operations, considering the horizontal architecture required to obtain Level 4 is critical. Since this often extends beyond the immediate budget or project on the table, it is lost in thought, priority, and vision.

This is the challenge for designing and building the right architecture.

From a proceeding perspective, it might, of course, be a valid approach to start with one central element, even with one system like planning in the above example. But this needs to be part of a broader road map and a holistic architecture. Any digitally transformed business will have an architecture that includes multiple solution providers, different technologies for various process support requirements, data engineering needs, and so on. To not initially architect the house on paper is foolish.

To provide a simple analogy, we are not suggesting you define the interior design elements of the kitchen, guest bath, master suite, or any other room in your digital house. But rather, it would be good to understand the room layout, number of floors, and planned plumbing requirements before we start picking furniture patterns for the love seat.

> One system can leverage some functional integration but not process integration and certainly not business transformation.

If a system claims to, be careful not to get crushed by a monolith.

The ambition of this chapter is not to outline YOUR technical architecture for digital business process transformation exactly. That would take a degree of hubris. There are too many nuances to be considered even to fit a single model across companies within the same industry. There are patterns for sure, but the right design for YOUR company takes sweat equity.

Since every corporation has a highly individual landscape of systems and technologies, a legacy of building blocks that support the status quo, the answer for a to-be, future state architecture and even more the answer to the path toward a to-be, future state architecture is highly individual and needs a thorough concept.

What we want to do here is to provide guidance for your to-be architecture regarding three essential directions that need to be incorporated.

Architecture Triumvirate for e2e Process Integration

These three directions are addressing three architectural areas:

⇨ Data

⇨ Process supporting functionality

⇨ The link into the business process

Figure 13: The Architecture Triumvirate

Data Decoupling

No doubt, the topic of data is one that is contaminated with **buzz-words**, including:

Data Lake

Data Warehouse

Data Fabric

Digital Twin

You will easily find more.

Let's stay free from buzzwords on an architectural level here. Let's build on two assumptions that can be assumed valid for most cases, for most corporations except for rare exceptions.

Assumption No. 1:

Source data is typically spread across many data sources, including bespoke systems. These are transactional systems like ERP, functional domain systems like warehouse management (WMS), transportation management (TMS), yard management (YMS) or alike in non-supply-chain environments, business partner data across suppliers, customers, distributors, and other parties, data streams like point-of-sale data, machine or product data from sensor device (Internet of Things, IoT), external big data streams like weather data, traffic data, and other unstructured data elements.

And, of course, let's not forget about our Excel files.

Heterogeneity is normality. Data from different sources is structurally and semantically different.

Assumption No. 2:

Any holistically defined scope for digital business process transformation will — as already explained — contain a multitude of different use cases. Many of the use cases may have commonalities regarding the required data from a content perspective. From a data structure perspective, use cases will often have different requirements. Either a solution for a use case has a given data model that needs to be fed, or the nature of use cases require different data structures, e.g., analytical vs transactional.

Diversity of use cases with commonality in data content is normality. As such, data structuring, data flow, and data harmonization are paramount.

There are basically two different strategies, and two architectural approaches to answer the data challenge. We call them *N to M* and *N to 1 to M* or *data decoupling* approach.

N to M

N to M means building direct links between all relevant source systems and all relevant target use cases. Given the fact that data from various sources is structurally and semantically heterogeneous, the necessary homogenization and logical contextualization need to be done several times.

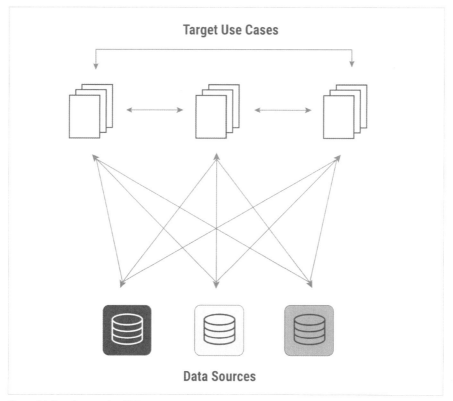

Figure 14. Data Integration N:M

This might be a favorable approach if both, the number of source systems and the number of target use cases, are and remain close to one each.

Since this is rather an exception than the rule, we usually recommend the decoupling or *N to 1 to M* approach.

N to 1 to M

The decoupling layer represents a structurally and semantically harmonized data layer. It's kept purpose-agnostic, i.e., is not yet converted into the structure or logic of the target use-cases, and intentionally homogenized generically.

Figure 15: Data Integration N:1:M

The purpose is to act as

1. a data quality proof point and catalyst,

2. a single source of truth, and

3. a data hub for all target use cases.

The decoupling approach does not only save time and effort by doing the generic homogenization once, but it also prevents differences that are unavoidable if this is done target use case by target use case. Regarding long-term benefits, it enables more rapid augmentation at the data harmonization layer and reduces risk and data rules, filters, and transformation logic changes to support additional use cases.

Taking into consideration that the business world keeps changing constantly, the decoupling approach has significant advantages in terms of time and effort, not only for the initial creation but particularly for ongoing maintainability and flexibility.

And a digitalized business and operating model needs to be kept up to date, otherwise, adoption erodes and turns back to tribal, faster than you think.

Composability

Composability as an innovative architectural approach is not an invention that we can claim for ourselves. It's a philosophy that Gartner raised and pushed for a while.[13] So, let's build on their foundation.

Gartner's notion of *Composability* refers to the ability to create and manage composite process-supporting solutions that are assembled from *loosely* coupled building blocks. This approach to technology solutions emphasizes the ability to build, modify, and integrate individual components in a flexible and modular manner, rather than relying on monolithic, tightly integrated systems.

Composability allows organizations to create and continuously adapt solutions that are tailored to their specific needs, while also reducing the time and cost associated with traditional solution development. By using pre-built, off-the-shelf components, organizations can quickly assemble solutions that meet their unique requirements, without having to build everything from scratch.

Composability also includes the ability to manage and maintain these composite solutions over time, making it easier to update and adapt to changing business needs. The use of loosely coupled components enables organizations to replace or modify individual components without affecting the overall solution, making it easier to respond to changing requirements and improve the overall solution over time.

---

13 "Becoming Composable: A Gartner Trend Insight Report," ID G00753614, Yefim Natis et al., published September 17, 2021

In summary, Gartner's notion of Composability is about the ability to create **flexible, modular, and adaptable technology solutions** that are tailored to specific business needs and can be easily updated and maintained over time.

While clearly foundational to our approach, we think that Gartner stops short on providing the answer in this element: What builds the backbone to orchestrate the composable elements? What is the logical frame to couple the building blocks *loosely*? We've got the answer, at least for the scope that we focus on.

Workflow Orchestration

The logical frame, the backbone that orchestrates the use of functional components, must be the business process. More specifically, it's the executable workflow.

The work of "digital workflow orchestration" is:

1. The explicit design of processes and workflows on the one hand, and

2. Linking the appropriate supporting functionality into the work-flow elements on the other, independent of whether it's functionality of source systems, new functionality for the specific target use case, or whether it's interactive functionality or an automation executed in the background, "traditional" or "smart" under use of AI, ML, optimization, or other advanced computing.

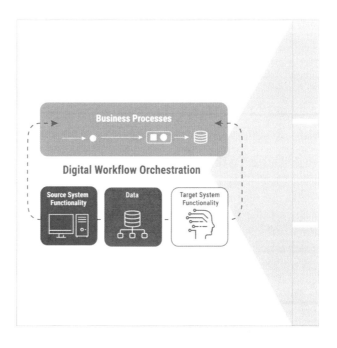

This results in executable workflows where the respective workflow actors — or automation where applicable — are triggered to contribute to the process as applicable. The workflow engine moves the "token", the process object, according to the business rules that are defined as an integral part of the workflow.

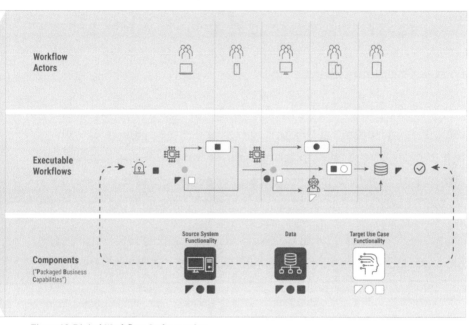

Figure 16: Digital Workflow Orchestration

The underpinning technologies must ensure the integrity of the information flow across workflow steps and assigned components of functionality.

Technology Selection

The technology stack of choice should enable digital business process transformation in a holistic, flexible, adaptable, responsive, and maintainable way, supporting the journey approach and not being built as a one-time "this is it!" A broad variety of capabilities across different layers and technologies is needed.

Our paradigms may tempt us to look for the jack of all trades in a single system. Unfortunately, this is also under the disguise of a single publisher who is really offering multiple disparate engines, data models, and workflows under the cover of a single user interface and invoicing party.

In fact, this idea that buying from one provider makes integration of data and processes easier, still remains one of the industry's leading fallacies — and an expensive one to boot. This is important:

> Attention — proprietary approaches that claim completeness for such a breadth of components and technologies are not the Holy Grail, but monoliths and, as such, dangerous.

A composite or quilted architecture may appear more complex at first glance, but it will provide much more flexibility, adaptability, and maintainability on a continuing basis.

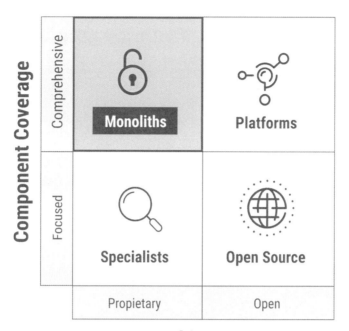

Figure 17: Quadrant of Architecture Paradigms

There is a relatively broad offering of solutions and products on the level of the single components. The decisive question is which characteristics are important; what enables the journey approach in a sustainable and maintainable way?

This leads to five important characteristics for the technology selection process.

Five Characteristics of the Technology Selection Process

1. Perfect "Fit Into Place"

The technical embedment into the individual starting position with value-add is important. Avoid "rip and replace" since it typically doesn't bring much incremental value. Technical openness and offering of synapses to other elements and components is crucial. Full stack environments and monoliths usually enforce redundancies to existing components and distract.

Build on what exists, complete what is missing and needed and tie everything together. This is the one time we will suggest and even recommend driving innovation at the edge, provided it is aligned with the future holistic vision, road map, and architecture. Getting wins early on your digital transformation journey, through selecting perfect fit solutions, is the greatest accelerant and momentum sustainer for the transformation and change journey.

2. Workflow Centricity

Appreciating workflow as the integration backbone is a new paradigm, very different from classical expert or dashboard-heavy applications. In addition to components needed for workflow design and execution orchestration, all components of the technology stack need to support this embedment and orchestration philosophy.

Composability, otherwise known as connecting the dots, is not only a conceptual mindset but also means light technical integrability by design. This is an essential non functional requirement.

3. Proximity to Business

There's a strong trend to democratize technology, to get non-technical process people involved in the creation of business solutions by opening access to "IT laymen" who don't have all the advanced technology skills and expertise. This trend strengthens for good reason: business requirements on the practicable level of executable workflows are not only complex, but they also constantly evolve and change.

Deep business process insight is key. The sustainability of any solution and adaptability to shifts in business dynamics is dependent on business engagement. That makes the pseudo-technical business leader invaluable in this digital industrial revolution.

Not implementing innovations, changes, and improvements in a timely manner is poison for adoption and a breeding ground for (new) tribal ways of working.

4. Low Lock-in

Using industry standards like Business Process Model and Notation (BPMN) for workflow modeling for example, as well as technically established standards, being open to integrating with libraries, open source, and external other sources is much smarter than expecting everything as proprietary built-in capability. Keep an eye on the lock-in effect.

No lock-in is not realistic when using third party components but keep it low.

5. Cost-Value Balance

Nowadays, many vendors demand huge, front-loaded investments into their technologies or systems, which creates a stretch between cost and return on value. An open, composite architecture will put you in a strong position to avoid this effect and strive for value-based part-nerships. There are also contractual negotiating tactics that can help allow you to "grow" into the system and more critically assure the ROI through the journey.

The architecture for the technological enablement of end-to-end transformed and integrated processes need to acknowledge three facts:

⇨ **PROCESS** is the new end-to-end integration backbone.

⇨ **DATA**, end-to-end integrated, harmonized, and contextualized, is its foundation.

⇨ **CHANGE** of business conditions and resulting requirements is the only constant and requires the highest adaptability and flexibility.

This is the **new true north**.

The People Side of the Equation — Creating Momentum

People are and will always be the heart of organizational innovation and transformation.

Barring extreme exceptions, we have never seen technology be the real hit-or-miss factor of transformations. Instead, it comes down to one thing.

PEOPLE

At the beginning of the book, we expressed the two factors that determine the success of digital transformation in a straightforward formula:

*Digital Effectiveness = Digital Enablement * Digital Adoption*

Adoption is the hit-or-miss factor.

Adoption is the result of changed behaviors — the practical acceptance of new ways of working. This brings us straight to the topic of change management.

We spoke about the superficiality of buzzwords earlier and the risk of different individual understandings remaining undetected when using such terms without definition.

So, let's first explain what we mean by *Change Management.*

> Change management refers to the process of managing the transition from a current state to a desired future operating model, to new ways of working for a defined scope of an organization.

It involves identifying, planning, implementing, and monitoring changes to processes, systems, technologies, or structures within an organization to achieve defined objectives.

Specifically for business process transformation, it must include the right skilling of the impacted people within the organization. Beyond that, it takes persistent monitoring for deviations from the designed workflow.

There are six building blocks of change management

1. Assessment

There needs to be a change assessment. This is a thorough analysis of the current state of the organization to determine the need for change and to identify the potential impacts of the change.

2. Communication

There needs to be appropriate communication from the start of the initiative well past the implementation and go-live dates. The development and execution of a communication plan to keep stakeholders informed about the change and to build support and buy-in for the change.

3. Planning

Failing to plan is planning to fail, especially when it comes to change management. The development of a road map for the change journey is required. This includes everything from timelines and budgets to resources and communication strategies.

4. Implementation

What is the actual execution of the change? Leaders must think through this, including but not limited to the design, development, and deployment of new processes, systems, and structures.

5. Training

With new technology and processes comes a new way of working. The development and delivery of training programs for employees, managers, and stakeholders to help them understand and adapt to the change.

6. Monitoring and Evaluation

There must be ongoing monitoring and evaluation of the change to assess its impact and effectiveness, resulting in any necessary adjustments to ensure its success.

Many say that the goal of change management is to minimize disruption and ensure that the change is smoothly and successfully implemented, while also maximizing the benefits and outcomes of the change for the organization and its stakeholders. But, if we're being perfectly candid, the real goal of change management is to **ensure the return on investments** in process reengineering and technology deployment is **realized through user adoption**.

Now, let's change perspective from the academic overview and try to see change management through the lens of those who are asked to adopt: the process users.

The most critical aspect of change management is to get these people confident, comfortable, and excited about operating in the new ways of working. The methodology to get there stands on three interrelated pillars.

Ownership

Education

Comfort

Three Pillars to Creating Adoption Momentum

Ownership

Ownership is created by involving the future process users in the design process. Obviously, not everyone can be part of the design team. Even so, playback sessions can create involvement, probably in a cascaded way, starting from higher-level concepts and going stepwise down to the day-to-day level.

A targeted endpoint might be the process users playing back the workflow and its supporting tools to their leaders and the program team. People will always lean to support that which they helped create. Pride of ownership is often undervalued.

Education

Education is, of course, closely associated with training but also relates to ownership.

The first process users being trained are those you want to sign off on new ways of working, to undergo the user acceptance test (UAT) where tools are involved. UAT and sign-off stage gates are often degraded to a technical exercise where it's tested that data gets into a system and functionality is workable. That's not enough! It needs to be proven that the process user is fully equipped to execute the operational workflow.

If you involve these process users early on, if you get their involvement, convey know-how, and get their feeling of ownership, you do not only have people who can sign off but also people who can teach others. They will, in essence, be influencers within their teams.

Just as in academia, the best test of understanding and proficiency is the ability to teach the concepts to one's peers. It is why the best students at university were always the Teacher Assistants or ran peer study groups.

Comfort

The pillar Comfort spans much broader and goes into the phase after sign-off and launch, deep into the real-life operations.

Besides the concept of continuous learning, durable comfort needs mainly two things to be sustainable.

On the one hand, there needs to be a continuous exchange between those who carry out the operational process and those who can shape and influence it. This emanates into the basic concept of continuous improvement, which we discuss in the next chapter.

On the other hand, the process users need a point of contact for questions — a kind of process support that can take the perspective of the operational person and help quickly. If users do not feel supported or are unsure of the right way to solve something, human ingenuity creeps in, and with it — tribal workflows.

What's the value of the nicest, fastest, newly constructed race car if you hand the keys to an inexperienced, unqualified, probably resistant driver? **Change management is key!**

However, as discussed in the *Pitfalls* section in Part II, the expectation of what change management can achieve and contribute should not be overstretched. It will help to make the change process smoother. You need to do the right things in the right sequence and embed change management into your road map from idea to launch of a transformed to-be-state and beyond.

In the aforementioned definition of change management, it was contained, but just summarized under *Implementation*, and we think it's worth a deeper look. Let's use our magic formula that we like to summarize the process from idea to launch in brief, as a structure to explain *Implementation*:

Think Big. Start Small. Scale Fast.

Think Big — From Idea to Vision

We spoke about the inherent dilemma of inventing a visionary future state, a new operating model without having experienced the game-changing power of digital enablement, without having done it already.

Uncharted waters.

In this early stage, it is important to create an environment for innovation — to give bandwidth for brainstorming, time for exploration, and some budget for trial and error.

We encourage sacrificing perfection for speed to test and course correct. There is time and place for perfection later.

Create an incubator for innovation, a small team as the nucleus for your digital business process transformation.

To **think big** is not just to focus on fixing current pain points. Take a moment to sketch out a big picture — the vision of what you want to achieve, not yet constraining how you technically want or could achieve it.

Start from the end, and apply backwards thinking.

Consider starting this big-picture development with a brainstorming and ideation workshop. No doubt that it needs some smart minds with good understanding of the scoped business area and visionary power, paired with imagination and/or experience in digital enablement.

Look for these smart minds internally and externally.

Having a solid draft of a big picture and of a vision for an outlined scope that you feel comfortable with to take you far enough to be transformative marks the milestone that transitions into the next phase.

Start Small — From Vision to New Operating Model

The next challenge is to shape the new operating and process model.

At this point, you will likely want to expand the nucleus team and pull some key brains out of their operational business role.

Be consistent and pull them out full time. Backfill internally or externally and free them up so they can prioritize the transformation. **These people will be your first ambassadors when they feel they've helped to create the future — evangelists for change.** Not to be redundant, but remember the old adages saying that people will always support that which they help create.

In reviewing 130 of our historical projects, those that started with a dedicated target operating model were delivered 73 percent more on time and 94 percent more likely to be within three percent of the budget. More importantly, the adoption rate for these programs exceeded 90 percent. That's far above the industry baseline. Additionally, they had a 92 percent net promoter score (NPS) score (industry leading is 74%).

So, the new operating model is probably the most important, the most far-reaching step on your transformation journey. Keep in mind that it's not about technology in the first instance; it's not about systems. **Think strictly from the perspective of the process and business side**. Develop a new process and interaction model, starting from a high level and going deeper step by step. As you gain depth, start to consider roles and accountabilities and project those onto the necessary organizational structure.

Even though the perspective should be process and not technology, new technologies usually play an essential role in figuring out the new operating model. In this case, consider little explorative pilot projects as part of this journey stage.

Having a solid description of the new operating and process model will not only help you to determine the size of the monster in terms of change but also to draft a first program road map and sketch the architecture in terms of data and types of systems and technology needed.

Scale Fast — From New Operating Model to Program to Launch

This is the typical program and project phase. We don't want to put much focus on program management essentials, you may have this competence in your organization already, and there are many books out there focusing specifically on this topic.

Apart from the essential precursor to this phase, developing an aspirational vision for a horizontal scope and transferring this into a new operating model, we just want to reiterate some essential aspects to be considered and kept alive in the way you set up and execute your program:

⇨ Organize the program outside of the line organization. Assign it to a hierarchical level that is above the functions contained in the scope. It's the C-level? Doesn't matter! That's the only way.

⇨ Free up program people from their operational roles. Backfill the positions internally or externally. One cannot be dedicated to working **on** the business if daily fires bring you back to working **in** the business constantly.

⇨ Take care that process centricity, detailed process work and change management don't get pushed aside. System-centric paradigms will kick in, as well as usual RFP dynamics. These need to be actively managed and counterbalanced.

⇨ The mandatory objective is that process users are able to operate in the newly designed ways of working with comfort, confidence, and excitement. Don't allow budget and time pressure — that will expectably come at some point — to compromise this objective.

The aforementioned aspects of change management need to be appropriately applied throughout the *Think Big — Start Small — Scale Fast* journey. Communication, socializing ideas and concepts, and the sparking of enthusiasm while managing expectations are the most important elements of change management in the early journey stages to create good momentum.

Going through this process and reaching the launch is by far not the end, but just a major milestone. To keep the good momentum and to make the digital business process transformation successful in the sense of being adopted and effective, it takes much more than the launch, the go-live, and the moment of deployment.

A digital transformation needs strategies to sustain the change. To point this out and to emphasize the essential importance, we have dedicated a separate chapter to **Strategies to Sustain the Change**.

Strategies to Sustain the Change

The operating model, the processes, the workflows, and the supporting tools need to be kept up to date, or adoption starts to erode, and tribal ways of working get a second wind and flourish again.

Earlier we touched on the risk of initial launch of frustration and losing mindshare of process users on their beginning adoption journey as one of the most common and irreversible pitfalls. It's not just about the necessary refinements and completions after the first wave of deployment, after the first launch of a new operating model. It is more about the fact that the business and surrounding environment are in a state of constant change.

We have seen this in *Health Check* engagements on digital transformation undertakings a few years after their start. Stakeholders, often CEOs or CFOs, have concerns or doubts about the continued value delivery of transformation investments that they have made previously. The tool was deployed, yet business results have been hard to confirm.

During the health check process, we typically find — when we measure adoption in some planning transformations — that execution adherence is less than 35 percent. I.e., nearly two thirds of all activities deviate from the explicitly designed way of working. So, apart from the fact that "Planning and Execution Control" was apparently a blind spot in their original, primarily vertical scope, something must have happened between launch and now.

May it be exogenous changes, may it be new institutional knowledge, may it be the drain of knowledge with people leaving or moving on, may it be that it was poor ever since and nobody measured — it apparently didn't get detected, analyzed, and fixed.

Such a health check and its outcomes are by far not the worst thing that can happen. A typical dynamic says, "everything is broken; we need to re-implement or replace the existing tools." However, the fact of the matter is that it is rarely the fault of the supporting tools or technologies. In most cases, the capability of owned technology is by far not exhausted.

Someone's got to be to blame and it's easiest to blame the system. But if that's the scapegoat, then the real mistake that was made is about to be repeated: the missing mechanisms to sustain the change.

From our experience, we recommend five strategic elements in combination to make sure that a transformational initiative gets sustainable traction and fundamentally changes the ways of working to deliver continued value.

5 Strategic Elements

These five elements include:

1. Changing the incentive structure from functional to end-to-end
2. Building a "Center of Excellence" from the onset
3. Measuring adoption as input for continuous improvement
4. Investing in a supportive setup over time
5. Choosing enabling tools and architecture for adaptability

Incentive Structure

It's given leadership wisdom that incentives drive — at least influence — behavior. Not everyone is altruistic enough to put the right decision over the individually more beneficial decision. Even if they are, who are they to question the metrics that management decided were important.

We once proposed a postponement concept in a pharmaceutical plant with a high, double-digit million-dollar savings potential. The plant was producing pharmaceutical end-consumer products in the form of tablets, predominantly for the European and Middle East market. The products were held in stock on the packaged finish goods level.

For the many countries with local packaging, package insert, languages, etc., this was creating an unbelievable value of inventory on hand, while many of the different packaged product variants contained the same tablets. The concept was to keep the stock on the unpackaged level, a so-called bulk product.

At the end of the presentation, the Executive Director and Head of manufacturing said, "This is an amazing concept. Someone should take this into consideration. Thank you!"

He stood up and left the room.

I was bewildered.

I couldn't get it out of my head to find out why the topic wasn't questioned but still dripped off him.

In the end, the answer was as simple as it was shocking.

Finished goods inventory was under accountability of sales, while production-related inventory was under accountability of manufacturing. Our proposal made perfect sense from a holistic, enterprise perspective, but from a functional perspective, it was creating an advantage for sales while at the expense of manufacturing.

> Incentives drive behavior. Functional incentives drive functional, siloed behavior.

We already outlined that transforming end-to-end means transitioning from a culture of functional optimization to one of enterprise-wide, cross-silo optimization. You need to adapt the incentive structure for all parties involved in the respective end-to-end scope accordingly; otherwise siloed thinking and optimization will continue.

One such tactic we have seen deployed successfully is a **shared metrics scorecard** across all functional senior leadership. This enables an honest conversation around trade-offs that involve inherently conflicting performance metrics.

Center of Excellence

Another key area to cater for sustaining transformational change starts at the very beginning: planning your support center.

It is about setting up a Center of Excellence (CoE) or whatever name might be appropriate, probably Centralized Digital Transformation Team, Continuous Improvement Team, etc. The nomenclature matters not; the presence and responsibility are critical to success and sustainment.

The concept is essentially identifying people who have strong social capital within the organization for evangelism and for innovation, who have functional knowledge about the scoped business area, but who also bring freethinking and outside-the-box mentality to innovate disruptively. But they should also find value in bringing concepts to life and supporting, fine tuning, and continuously improving a new operating model.

This team should be implanted at the beginning of the digital adoption journey. Their goal should be to ensure that the people they represent via business function, business unit, and geographical region feel as if their voices are consistently heard, and their input is consistently reintegrated into the process.

That feedback needs to be reintegrated into the organization and operating model design as well as into the tools and technology. In some rare but successful case studies, companies have even changed the incentive structure of this team to be entirely dependent on adoption, net promoter score (NPS), and satisfaction surveys of the process user community.

This team is not created for the initial phase only; this team is built to stick around.

Measure Adoption

For transformational initiatives, you typically build a business case on factors that impact working capital, profit and loss, and customer service.

What we often see lacking is the upfront definition of key metrics on how to measure process adherence and user adoption at the onset.

But this aspect is twofold, and the definition and establishment of such measurements is only one aspect. The more important one is the purpose, the consequence you have in mind when measuring.

Our recommendation is to not use metrics for punishment but for the intent of identifying areas for continuous improvement and further training. So, you may see individuals stepping outside of the process, offline from the to-be path and doing something on their own; you detect, for example, a microcosm of Excel workbooks or little offline tools.

The tenor of the subsequent discussion should not be "misbehavior got detected" but rather "opportunities for improvement have been found." This is a subtle but materially critical difference in approach. Assume a good reason for the deviation and not a bad intention by default.

A great conversation approach that we've witnessed is something like this:

> *Hey, I love the fact that you're continuously trying to drive improvement in the process, and you're finding innovative ways to solve things in addition to the tool and the process as designed and deployed so far.*

> *To accommodate for a way to ensure that you're driving that level of success and innovation across the whole organization and making your life easier, it would be great for us to understand how we can get what you're doing to be incorporated into the standard process and supported by further tool enablement to better support you in fulfilling the business needs.*

With this approach, you are coming from a place of understanding and praise which will open the door for a constructive discussion to find out what's needed. Sometimes it is just training; sometimes it is refinement or enhancement. Either way, it will improve and sustain adoption.

Supportive Setup

The day-to-day business and expectations from internal and external stakeholders keep process users continuously under high pressure. This is a matter of fact, independent of where you are on your transformational journey. Accept that this fact creates the necessity to provide a supportive setup. The setup changes over time, but the necessity does not disappear.

We discussed the transformational phase from initiation to launch in the chapter before, so let's focus on post-launch here. We are distinguishing two phases:

1. Getting started after launch.
2. Ongoing operations.

In fact, there is no clear line between these phases; it is more of a continuous progression. But let's stick with the distinction for the sake of simplification.

To get started, we see more and more companies taking temporary advantage of third-party partners, who can supplement and augment their operational team. These partners consist of people having operational experience within an operating model that is similar to what the company is striving to achieve at the end of the transformation.

This approach has materialized several positive effects for those case studies reviewed across the interviews we conducted.

It provides some additional capacity to handle the unchanged pressure of the day-to-day business, and it avoids the instantaneous reflex of falling back into old habits. The operational people have more time to learn, apply, adopt, gain proficiency, and accelerate.

It provides experience and go-to expertise for a direct, immediate approach inside the operational process.

It also demonstrates to people inside and outside the team, particularly those in the Mighty Middle, to see that the way how the vision has been operationalized is workable.

Regardless of how much change management you have applied and how smart it was, you will always have some people who are just observing and waiting for the moment to say, "*Look, it doesn't work. I've said this from day one.*"

Staff augmentation and supplementation of executing in the new ways of working will help to neutralize some of that passive resistance.

The more your organization and your people develop a routine and adopt new ways of working, the more you approach a state of ongoing operations, the more the challenge will shift toward staying up to date.

The business changes constantly and incredibly fast. Change in the macroeconomic conditions, in the competitive environment, new ways to market, new product launches, new business strategies, and new priorities — change is the only constant.

Missing out on identifying these changes and their impact on the operating mode, processes, workflow, and supporting tools will make the newly implemented operating model antiquated very quickly.

Under the pressure of the day-to-day, process users will quickly find alternatives — means work-arounds — to solve an urgent problem at hand. Erosion starts with the first bit but quickly develops a progressive dynamic. The tipping point where your new model is outdated and trumped by new tribal ways of working happens surprisingly early.

The only way to prevent this dynamic from happening is to continue your CoE, or whatever name you've used, as an integral part of the new operating model and organization. This will enable accountability, authority, skilled capacity, and budget to keep the operating model, processes, workflows, and supporting tools in line with changing business requirements.

You may want to choose a blended team of internal and external resources, probably shifting more and more from external to internal and using the external arm for peaks, for special requirements, as a sounding board and critical pair of eyes.

The important thing is less how you organize it but that you cater for it. And it needs to be at speed and scalable. It is and continues to be a race that you don't want to lose.

Adaptive Tools and Architecture

Quick adaptability to changes and to new requirements is not only a design principle for the supporting organization but even more for the architecture of data, tools and technology that enable the operating model.

The times, when tools were built for generations, are over. The lever for integration — as explained in the chapters before — is not a system anymore, but rather data and process. Being able to provide data as needed from a single source of truth without doing long-lasting integration projects is key.

Same as being able to respond to new business requirements swiftly by providing appropriate support with the means of the technology stack that fits best. Horizontal integration and embedment into the workflow happen through digital workflow orchestration where needed.

Ideally, the architectural design, as well as the tools and technologies that are selected as part of the enablement stack, allow and support democratized approaches of configuring, designing, and building supporting functions.

Democratization of information technology is about opening access to people who do not have all the advanced skills and/or training of IT specialists. It's often called *citizen access*, as it gives means to business process users which were reserved for IT people before.

This allows for establishing the continuous improvement process in proximity to and under authority of business to avoid long change request approval cycles with IT organizations. These are simply not set up for continuous support and journey-type engagements.

Design and selection of enablement architecture and technology are essential determining factors for the ability to sustain the change. Therefore, speed of adaptability and flexibility to react to changes and to new requirements at the speed of business need to be key criteria for design and selection.

Conclusion

Get it right, or leave it. Anything else is waste.

Money, time, energy invested for nothing.

Let's start with a blunt question.

Do you really want to TRANSFORM, or do you just want to RENOVATE your selected scope of business processes?

In case it's the latter, let's say you digitalize a specific information process by implementing an integrated system to replace home grown tools, as an example; that's absolutely fine, provided you don't expect transformative results.

Transformation is not incrementally improving an as-is state. Transformation is reengineering. It's about rethinking and redesigning a new operating model for a scope that is defined holistically enough to create a positive impact for customers and shareholders.

Digital transformation is a transformation that makes use of digital enablement to facilitate a defined new operating model, taking care of all prerequisites and surrounding conditions to make it sustainably adopted and effective. It breaks down the new operating model from business purpose to processes to operational workflows to supporting technology and educates the human actors to play their roles.

Digital transformation is not just applying digital enablement and expecting a transformed operating model as a result.

Putting an organization on a genuinely transformational path takes much more than just prominently declaring an initiative or software implementation project to be a transformation. It needs top management initiative and attention to prevent a transformative approach from falling back into traditional patterns. There are too many paradigms and organizational habits that will get applied automatically if not actively neutralized.

Twelve imperatives

Here are twelve imperatives that are essential to lay the foundation for successful digital business process transformation.

1. Put a Vision Ahead

It helps the entire organization to understand *why*. It might be crystal clear to some, but don't miss the chance to make it tangible for everyone and drive alignment from the start. You either need a vision or a burning platform as a motivation, a purpose for your organization to open up for change.

Don't explain *how*. Apply Simon Sinek's, *Start with WHY*.

2. Beyond Hierarchies

Inventing a truly transformative, reengineered operating model requires the freedom to move beyond functional boundaries, locations, and established organizational dimensions. However, these are exactly the dimensions that are usually reflected in the given organizational structure.

Conversely, this means quite simply that real cross-silo and end-to-end thinking can only happen in a setup beyond given hierarchies.

3. Holistic Scope

A transformational scope needs to be broad and comprehensive enough to create an impact on customers and/or shareholders. But often, initiatives just take a vertical focus on a specific business function, typically related to the functional scope of a system or software category. The horizontal, cross-functional interconnection with other business functions is often kept out of scope but is essential.

4. Calibrate Management Expectations

Disappointment starts with expectations. C-sponsors need to understand that it will take longer than they wish, it will cost more than they are told, and any magic promise to make it quick and cheap will, in fact, cost x-times more later and make real transformation only more elusive.

5. Proactively Manage the Mighty Middle

Identify the Mighty Middle, the Clay Layer in your scope. Manage the few individuals with massive power by being the center of tribal decision processes today. Acknowledge that digital transformation is their natural enemy.

Whatever *manage* might mean, winning them to lead the change, moving them into other positions outside scope, use outplacement in case. But do it proactively, as a preparatory activity to build the foundation for transformational change.

6. Process-led, Not Technology-led

Ensure that a new operating and process model exists before systems and technology get selected. The misbelief that a system inherently brings the process, and a new operating model emerges as a result, is widespread. Buzzwords and the transformation-suggesting language of system providers do their part to equate "system" and "solution."

Overcome the paradigm that a system is the backbone of your transformed to-be state. The new operating model is the backbone; technology and systems are just enablers.

7. Take the Workflow Perspective

The new operating and process model needs to be facilitated on the level where the work flows. That's where the operational day-to-day happens.

All relevant details count. It's irrelevant whether a requirement is covered by out-of-the.box functionality of a tool or not if the workflow needs it. Be strict on the workflow perspective and flexible on how to support the necessary technically.

8. Preparedness for the Data Challenge

Transforming a holistic scope requires integration across a holistic business context. This contextualization enforces holistic data quality, while for digitalization of fragments, partial quality is good enough.

The new operating model and its processes and workflows being the backbone of the transformed to-be, integrated data of decent contextualized quality and reliability is the foundation.

9. Prepare beyond Project Phase from the Start

In dynamic business environments, nothing is as constant as change. All elements of a new, digitally integrated operating model — people, process, data, tools — need to be kept up to date, and constantly adapted. It's not only about the big changes, but about all relevant changes, also small ones. Otherwise, the digital operating model starts to erode and falls back to tribal state quickly.

10. Calibrate the Role of Change Management

Classical change management means are important to support transformational change. But they cannot compensate for the omission of detailed workflow design. Executable processes and workflows are the most important instrument of change management as such. Classical change management is the lubricant.

11. Caution with Vendors and "Advisors"

Be cautious with software vendors and system integrators who call themselves consultants or advisors.

Software/technology vendors are not interested in transformation, even when their marketing language says differently. Given their SaaS-based business model, they just want to sell as big and as quickly as possible. Many "advisors" act as vendors' extended arm in an agnostic consultant's costume during the process. Even as such, they are biased system integrators rather than agnostic. They are, candidly speaking, neither objective nor experienced in true transformation.

12. Counterbalancing the Mechanisms of RFPs

Ensure the presence of a strong advocate who actively defends the need for detailed process-work, change management etc. — both cost time and money. In any competitive vendor selection process where technology or software implementation is involved, these aspects will be cut out.

Separate process work and change management from system implementation as much as possible. They need different skills and mindsets, anyway.

None of these imperatives will happen by just telling your organization to do so. It needs powerful, persistent steering from the top. Based on these principles, you can start building your transformational "race car."

The Path to Success

Let's briefly summarize *The path toward successful digital business process transformation* into some construction guidelines for building your transformational "race car."

The big picture is outlined for a comprehensive, horizontally shaped end-to-end scope, converted into an exciting vision that underlines the transformative ambition and magnitude by addressing the impact on external stakeholders.

Probably the most important, the most far-reaching step on your entire transformation journey needs to be addressed at the very beginning:

Inventing, developing, and thoroughly designing the new operating model.

Skipping this step is the most common mistake made in digital business process transformation.

Keep in mind that it's not about technology in the first instance; it's not about systems. Think strictly from the perspective of the process and business side. Develop a new process and interaction model, starting from a high level and going deeper step by step. With gaining depth, start to consider roles and accountabilities and project it also onto the necessary organizational structure to support.

Even though the perspective should be process and not technology, new technologies usually play an essential role in figuring out the new operating model. In this case, consider little explorative pilot projects as part of this journey stage.

> **The new operating model, with its processes and operational workflow, is the true object of digitalization. This is the backbone that technology must support, not the other way around.**

This is the basis from which you can derive the four important design fields of the transformation:

1. Assess the complexity of scoped process landscape and calibrate your transformational change approach.

    The more complex, cross-functional, decision-oriented processes with tribal, knowledge-based, not explicitly structured legacy are part of the scope, the more important it is to approach the change as a stepwise journey without striving for complete automation straight away.

    Our *Maturity Model* — see Part III, page 181 ff. — gives guidance in this respect.

2. Lay out the technical architecture for data and technologies to support the transformational scope.

    Your transformational scope will need support from various systems, technologies, and tools. If one system could cover your scope, be sure your scope for digital transformation is too short sighted, too vertical, and not holistic and will lead to system implementation, not transformation.

Systems are not the backbone anymore to integrate and digitally transform. **Kill this paradigm.**

The new integration backbone is the new operating model and its processes, supported by scope-wide integrated data.

Three essentials your technology architecture should cover are:

⇨ A data-decoupling strategy with a generically harmonized single source of truth in the center.

⇨ A stack of technologies and systems that support the notion of composability.

⇨ Digital workflow orchestration to link data, tools, and technology into digitally orchestrated processes and workflows.

3. Calibrate the change management needed in-program to achieve and post-program to sustain adoption.

People are and will always be the heart of innovation and transformation. Your change management approach needs to create ownership, education, and comfort. Effective, adopted transformation is not about successfully passing user tests or go-live stage gates; it is about equipping the process users to execute the operational workflow to live the new operating model.

The strategy to sustain a transformational achievement is imperative to be planned from the onset. Since the only guaranteed constant in business is change, you need to keep your new operating model up to date. Furthermore, the transformation has been intentionally approached as a journey, so continuous improvement is key.

Measurement, capacity, and organization, the design of your enabling architecture to remain adaptable, all is ideally premeditated from the very beginning.

4. Build the road map and plan for time, capacity, budget, and return.

Well, yes. A real transformation will take much longer than a system implementation. And yes, it is more costly. It is more challenging to nail the return. But the return will not only be higher and incomparably more sustainable in the mid and long run.

It's the only way to grasp the digital age.

Let's get to the point. It is harsh, yet true.

**Get it right, or leave it. Anything else is waste.
Money, time, energy invested for nothing.**

The worst thing we have seen several times — not an exception, but rather a pattern — is the following dynamic.

A big initiative starts, probably called a transformation, but approached in the traditional way and, in the end, not much more than a massive system implementation with the specialty of being enormously costly with a multi-million-dollar budget associated.

Expectations are transformative; the scope is rather vertical, and the focus lies on system capabilities; process work and change management were stripped off in the RFP cycle. Hence, the operating model, processes, and workflows are elaborated — best case and only within the vertical scope — on a superficial "blueprint" level.

Consequently, things evolve as predicted:

Tribal f*cks up digital.

Poor adoption. Little impact.

Now the blame game starts. And typically, it takes a dynamic that ends with blaming the system for not being capable enough. Sometimes, especially in cases where the system and vendor selection were already political infighting, the original losing party comes out and says, "You see, our choice would have been better."

We've seen tens of millions of dollars in investments fall into the abyss with the wise decision to do the same thing again with a different system. **What a waste! What stupidity!**

Regardless of where you are on your transformational journey, pre-, in-, or post-program, it's never too late to take influence and to course-correct.

Yes, it may take more time and more money than originally planned. But be assured, the return on investment will be incomparably higher than letting it go and doing nothing.

It's time to shift paradigms.

It's time to approach digital business process transformation in the right way. It's time to strive for sustainable adoption and effectiveness to stay ahead of the competition.

Yes, it requires courage to fight paradigms and go against the mainstream.

YOUR courage.

YOU can be the **crystal nucleus** in your organization.

It's your Kairos, your decisive moment.

If you have the power, then start now. If you don't, start now to look for allies.

We'd love to support you with *Privileged Access to Supporting Resources* in the final chapter, taking your stage of journey — pre, in, post — into consideration.

Privileged Access to Supporting Resources

Thank you for purchasing your copy of *Tribal F*cks up Digital*. We wrote this book with a lot of commitment and dedication to giving digital business process transformation a positive spin toward success.

We see so much wasted time, energy, creativity, and money, when proven tactics can be used to avoid it. These resources are typically invested in fundamentally correct projects, but we see things repeatedly stumbling with the same common pitfalls.

Our motivation is to help YOU to make it better!

We hope that this book is already a first step for you. But we are committed to supporting you further and are offering **privileged access** to further resources to YOU as a reader.

What can you expect when using the subsequent QR-link?

- Downloadable versions of the graphics used in Part III
- Some questionnaires, checklists, and tools for self-assessment
- Pre-releases of blog articles, news, podcasts, etc.
- Exclusive opportunities and access to "Meet the Authors"
- and much more

About the Authors

Klaus Imping

Born in 1966 in Germany, with a universal education in Business Administration, I had almost a decade in various roles in the manufacturing industry before switching over to the consulting side. Working with numerous clients and projects for almost three

decades and always acting in the magic triangle of information technology, processes, and strategy. Many of my viewpoints come from focusing on supply chain management in a global context and being in C-level charge for more than a decade, leading as CEO since 2020.

This is my professional path. My driving force, however, relates to the professional path of my beloved dad, to whom I dedicate this book. He remained loyal to his first employer for almost forty years. A midsize company where he started his professional journey at the amazing age of fourteen. Textile industry, Germany. Success story in the 1960s and early 1970s. Then disruptive change evolved. When it hit my father's company unprepared, it was too late. Ten years of suffering business, ten years of creeping death — that I observed as a child and teenager — ended in the company's bankruptcy. I saw my father suffering. It was not his job and not his pay grade to initiate the turn. He was a victim, a passenger on a sinking ship.

My learnings: Become strong. Become independent. Once you sense things going wrong: stand up, articulate your opinion, and take action. If I am being honest, my dedication to "KAIROS" is also rooted in these learnings. KAIROS, the Greek god of the moment, known as the decisive moment, is the passing instant when an opening appears that must be seized with force if success is to be achieved. Taking influence, giving impulses, raising hands, and stating an opinion that is not mainstream — this is not possible without the decisive moment, without the small moment where you make the decision to act.

For me, the KAIROS sculpture is the perfect physical expression of this decisive moment, the power that it can unfold, and also the courage it takes to do so. "The point of power is always in the present moment," my good friend, mentor and longtime fellow Christian Zott once said to me. He's so right.

Michael Ciatto

Born in 1986 in Reading, PA, USA, to loving and supportive parents Kerry and Cindy Ciatto, I was not academically trained neither in supply chain nor engineering. Rather, I pursued Economics, with a specification in Finance, as well as Political Science during my time in academia at Dickinson College. Through the support of generous Sigma Chi alumni during his collegiate years, my interest in business was cultivated.

After entering the world of finance initially, the Great Recession of 2008 provided a career inflection point, and I pivoted into the world of consulting, starting with turnaround management. My role evolved into interim management with exposure to several roles, ranging from procurement, manufacturing, and logistics to corporate strategy.

My love of new ventures led me to accept a new challenge in the supply chain and digital transformation field, which was new to me. Lucky to have the trust of two mentors, Mike Landry and Karim Barkawi, I was eager to learn and advance quickly. After purchasing several books and boarding a flight to Italy for my first week on the job, my passion for Digitally Enabled Transformation was ignited. Since then, I have spent over a dozen years in the Supply Chain transformation space, most recently as the CEO of the Supply Chain Service Line.

Through countless client engagements, I have become a vocal advocate of the importance of people and operating models in unlocking value through digital and technology innovations. With my personal career being born through practical trial and error, I have learned that the most successful leaders and companies are willing to test hypotheses and encourage learning through failure.

I am convinced that it is genuinely important to approach all transformation engagements — despite how many engagements you might have under your belt — with the humility that there will always be a surprise or new learning.

Personally, my greatest satisfaction comes from partnering with people to unlock new learnings. That moment of understanding and enlightenment is the greatest reward of all. This is likely a gene I inherited from my parents and grandparents, who were all educators. Digital transformation journeys provide the opportunity for those moments of epiphany, improving the quality of life for all those involved, including the consumers of the products and services these enterprises provide.

Made in the USA
Monee, IL
22 May 2023

0a03042f-6060-49dc-9462-e0f0005699aaR01